AF251008

Table of Contents

Introduction

Have you ever wondered which diet is the perfect fit to meet all your health needs? Do you want to eat fresh, healthy meals without compromising on your health and the flavors? Then you need to switch to the 30 days whole food diet. The 30-day whole foods is a month-long clean-eating plan that promises a slew of physical and mental advantages. It was created in 2009 by two qualified sports nutritionists who touted it as a means to remodel your relationship with food and reset your metabolism. The diet is based on the notion that specific food types can have a negative impact on your health and fitness. As a result, eliminating these foods from your diet should aid your body in recovering from the harmful impacts and promoting long-term health. The majority of people appear to be following this diet with the hopes of losing weight.

Some people, on the other hand, may use the program to identify dietary intolerances or reap some of the program's health benefits. The 30- day whole food program's concept is simple: for 30 days, eliminates all items that may be harmful to your health.

After the first 30 days, gradually reintroduce the item you've missed, keeping track of how it affect your body. The diet contains a set of tight guidelines. It also includes a list of meals that are permitted as well as items that are prohibited. Cheating is not permitted during the month-long elimination stage. If you get off track, you'll have to restart the challenge from the beginning. According to the founders, strict adherence allows your body to reset by removing items that may trigger inflammation, gastrointestinal disruptions, or hormone imbalances. A morning walk may provide you with more energy throughout the day. This is especially true if you go for a walk outside. Adults who walked for 20 minutes outside had greater vitality and energy than those who walked for 20 minutes indoors, according to studies. For 18 sleep-deprived women, 10 minutes of stair walking was more energetic than a cup of coffee, according to tiny research. Try going for a walk the next time you need an energy boost in the morning or are tired when you wake up. Walking is the first thing in the morning that may assist you in achieving your weight loss goals. Walking for 30 minutes at a moderate pace can burn up to 150 calories. You might lose weight if you combine it with a healthy diet and strength training.

Many health benefits are supposed to come from sticking to the 30-day whole foods for 30 days. Fat loss, increased energy, better sleep, fewer food cravings, and greater sports performance are just a few of the benefits. Furthermore, the diet's creators claim that it will alter your perception of food as well as your taste. Diet supporters also say that it can change your emotional relationship with food and your body. Although these alleged benefits appear to be highly appealing, it's important to remember that there are currently no scientific studies to back them up.

Foods to Eat

30-day whole foods allows you to eat the following ingredients:
- ✓ Fish and seafood
- ✓ Meat and poultry
- ✓ Fruits
- ✓ Vegetables
- ✓ Nuts and seeds
- ✓ Eggs
- ✓ Fats: Plant oils, clarified butter, duck fat, coconut oil, and ghee.

When picking minimally processed foods, the diet recommends choosing those with the shortest ingredient lists and the fewest ingredients.

Foods to Avoid

Certain foods items are not suitable for this diet, such as:

☒ Sugar and artificial sweeteners: Raw sugar, honey, maple syrup, agave syrup and all products containing these sweeteners, as well as artificial sweeteners.

☒ Alcohol: All types of beer, wines, liqueurs and spirits.

☒ Grains: Regardless of their degree of processing, all grains, including wheat, corn, oats and rice, are to be avoided.

☒ Pulses and legumes: Most peas, lentils and beans, including peanut butter, should be avoided. Green beans, sugar snap peas and snow peas are exceptions.

☒ Soy: All soy, including tofu, tempeh, edamame and all products derived from soy, such as miso and soy sauce.

☒ Dairy: Including cow, goat and sheep's milk, yogurt, cheese, ice cream and other products derived from dairy. Clarified butter or ghee is allowed.

☒ Processed additives: These include carrageenan, MSG or sulfites. Any food or beverage containing these ingredients should be avoided.

On this regimen, there is no such thing as a cheat meal. Instead, you're urged to follow the rules to the letter at all times. If you do make a mistake, the diet's creators strongly advise you to start over from the beginning.

The Reintroduction Phase After 30-Day Whole Foods

It's time to focus on step 2: the reintroduction phase. Once you've completed the 30-Day Whole Foods program, certain foods will be gradually reintroduced during this phase to see how they affect your better metabolism, digestive tract, immune system, and connection with food. The recommended method for reintroducing off-limit foods is to do so one food group at a time. Milk, for example, can be reintroduced on day 1. On days 2–4, you should revert to the 30-day whole foods and avoid milk while keeping an eye on any potential symptoms.

Salad For Breakfast

Prep Time: 10 minutes.

Cook Time: 15 minutes.

Serves: 4

Ingredients:

- 1 pound pork breakfast sausage
- 9 eggs, hard-boiled
- 3 cups cherry tomatoes, halved
- ¼ cup purple onion, sliced
- 2 avocados, diced
- ½ cup fresh cilantro, chopped
- 1 teaspoon kosher salt
- ¼ teaspoon black pepper
- ¼ cup lemon juice

Preparation:

1. At 400 degrees F, preheat your oven.
2. Layer a baking sheet with parchment paper.
3. Make ½ inch meatballs out of the sausage and place them in the baking sheet.
4. Bake the meatballs for 15 minutes.
5. Mix eggs, lemon juice, black pepper, salt, cilantro, meatballs, avocado, onion and tomatoes in a bowl.
6. Serve.

Serving Suggestion: Serve the salad with bread and fried eggs.

Variation Tip: Add some black pepper for more taste.

Nutritional Information Per Serving:

Calories 312 | Fat 25g |Sodium 132mg | Carbs 4g | Fiber 3.9g | Sugar 3g | Protein 18.9g

Pizza Quiche

Prep Time: 15 minutes.

Cook Time: 25 minutes.

Serves: 8

Ingredients:

- 1 teaspoon ghee melted
- 8 large eggs
- ¼ cup coconut milk
- ½ teaspoon garlic powder
- ½ teaspoon onion powder
- ¼ teaspoon salt
- ½ teaspoon black pepper
- ¼ teaspoon dried oregano
- 1 ½ cups mushrooms sliced
- ½ cup roasted red pepper sliced
- 3 oz. pepperoni quartered
- ¼ cup green onions chopped
- 2 tablespoons pizza sauce

Preparation:

1. At 375 degrees F, preheat your oven.
2. Grease a 10 inch springform pan with cooking spray.
3. Beat eggs with coconut milk, oregano, black pepper, salt, onion powder and garlic powder in a bowl.
4. Stir in green onions, pepperoni, roasted red pepper and mushrooms.
5. Pour this mixture in the prepared pan and add the pizza sauce on top.
6. Bake for 25 minutes in the oven then slice.
7. Serve warm.

Serving Suggestion: Serve this quiche with crispy bacon.

Variation Tip: Add sautéed ground chicken or pork on top of eggs.

Nutritional Information Per Serving:

Calories 297 | Fat 15g |Sodium 548mg | Carbs 5g | Fiber 4g | Sugar 1g | Protein 19g

Sausage Balls

Prep Time: 15 minutes.

Cook Time: 43 minutes.

Serves: 6

Ingredients:

- 1 large sweet potato
- 1 tbsp. organic Dijon mustard
- ⅓ cup coconut flour
- 2 tbsp. organic butter
- 2 tbsp. chopped seasonings onion
- 2 tsp. Italian seasoning
- 2 large eggs
- sea salt and pepper, to taste
- 1 lb. pork sausage or chorizo

Preparation:

1. At 350 degrees F, preheat your oven.
2. Soak sweet potato in a bowl with ½ inch water, cover and steam for 8 minutes in the microwave.
3. Drain the cooked potatoes, peel and cut them into cubes.
4. Sauté sausage with seasonings, and mustard in a pan until brown.
5. Mash the potatoes in a bowl then add rest of the ingredients.
6. Take 2 teaspoons of this mixture to make a ball and make more balls in the same way.
7. Place these balls in the baking sheet and bake for 35 minutes in the oven.
8. Serve warm.

Serving Suggestion: Serve the ball with crumbled crispy bacon on top and fried eggs on the side

Variation Tip: Add some paprika for more spice.

Nutritional Information Per Serving:

Calories 134 | Fat 4.7g |Sodium 1mg | Carbs 4.1g | Fiber 7g | Sugar 3.3g | Protein 26g

Potato Boats

Prep Time: 15 minutes.

Cook Time: 65 minutes.

Serves: 2

Ingredients:

- 1 large potato
- 1 teaspoon olive oil
- generous amount of kosher salt and pepper

Preparation:

1. At 425 degrees F, preheat your oven.
2. Rub the potato with black pepper, oil and salt then place in the baking sheet.
3. Roast the potato for 65 minutes in the oven.
4. Cut the potato in half and top each half with a poached egg and avocado slices.
5. Serve warm.

Serving Suggestion: Serve the boats with bacon and bread.

Variation Tip: Drizzle red pepper flakes on top for a tangier taste.

Nutritional Information Per Serving:

Calories 217 | Fat 13g |Sodium 114mg | Carbs 3.1g | Fiber 1g | Sugar 10g | Protein 21g

Salmon Frittata

Prep Time: 15 minutes.

Cook Time: 38 minutes.

Serves: 12

Ingredients:

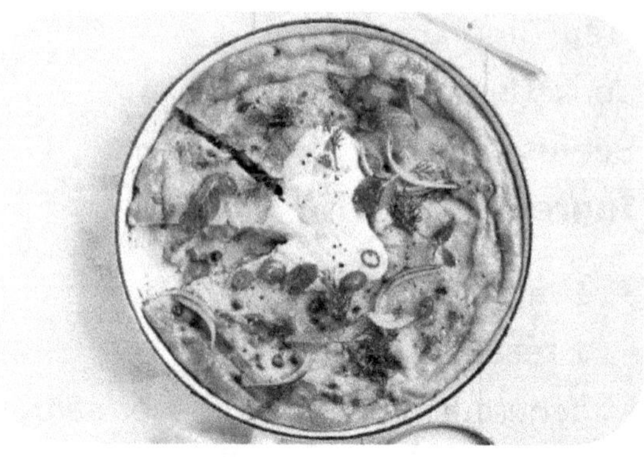

- 1.5 lbs. salmon
- 10 eggs
- ½ a small onion
- 2 tbsp. cooking oil
- 1 tbsp. chopped dill
- 1 tbsp. chopped capers
- 1 tsp. chopped chives
- Caper Dill Mayo
- salt and black pepper, to taste

Preparation:

1. Sauté salmon with oil, black pepper and salt in a skillet for 5 minutes.
2. Flip the salmon pieces and cook for 3 minutes then remove from the heat.
3. Beat eggs with black pepper, salt, chives, capers, and dill in a bowl.
4. Break the salmon pieces and add to the eggs.
5. Pour this salmon mixture in a greased baking pan.
6. Bake the eggs for 30 minutes in the oven.
7. Slice and serve.

Serving Suggestion: Serve the frittata

Variation Tip: Add chopped parsley to the egg mixture.

Nutritional Information Per Serving:

Calories 311 | Fat 12.5g |Sodium 595mg | Carbs 3g | Fiber 12g | Sugar 12g | Protein 17g

Kale Quiche With Sweet Potato Crust

Prep Time: 10 minutes.

Cook Time: 51 minutes.

Serves: 4

Ingredients:

- 2 mediums to large sweet potatoes
- half of a sweet onion
- 6 stalks of lacinato kale
- 1 small crown of broccoli
- 2 cloves of garlic
- 2 extra large eggs and 2 extra large egg whites
- 1 T miso {optional}
- 0.75 c shredded mozzarella
- big spoonful of goat cheese
- kosher salt and freshly-ground pepper

Preparation:

1. At 400 degrees F, preheat your oven.
2. Peel and pass the sweet potatoes through the mandolin.
3. Spread the sweet potato slices in a glass pie dish.
4. Bake this sweet potato crust for 15 minutes in the oven.
5. Reduce oven's heat to 375 degrees F.
6. Sauté onion with oil in a skillet for 5 minutes.
7. Stir in kale, and broccoli then cook for 5 minutes.
8. Add garlic and cook for 30 seconds.
9. Beat eggs in a bowl then add cheese and miso.
10. Fold in veggie mixture and pour this mixture over the sweet potato crust.
11. Bake the eggs for 30 minutes in the oven.
12. Slice and serve warm.

Serving Suggestion: Serve this quiche with crispy bread toasts.

Variation Tip: Add chopped potatoes to the eggs before baking.

Nutritional Information Per Serving:

Calories 212 | Fat 12g |Sodium 321mg | Carbs 4.6g | Fiber 4g | Sugar 8g | Protein 17g

Baked Breakfast Sweet Potatoes

Prep Time: 15 minutes.

Cook Time: 67 minutes.

Serves: 4

Ingredients:

- 2 medium sweet potatoes
- 4 slices bacon
- 1 medium sweet onion, diced
- 4 garlic cloves, minced
- sea salt and black pepper
- 4 small eggs

Preparation:

1. At 400 degrees F, preheat your oven.
2. Poke whole sweet potatoes with a fork and place them in a baking sheet.
3. Roast these sweet potatoes for 45 minutes in the oven.
4. Sauté bacon in a skillet until brown then transfer to a plate.
5. Sauté onion and garlic in the bacon grease for 7 minutes.
6. Crumble and add the bacon to the skillet.
7. Cut both the potatoes in half and scoop out the flesh from the center.
8. Add mashed sweet potato to the skillet, cover and cook for 10 minutes.
9. Stir in black pepper and salt then mix well.
10. Place the sweet potatoes in the in the baking sheet.
11. Divide the mash in the potato shells and make a well at the center.
12. Crack one egg in each sweet potato and bake for 15 minutes.
13. Serve warm.

Serving Suggestion: Serve the crispy potatoes with muffins on the side.

Variation Tip: Add some garlic salt or Sugar-free BBQ sauce to season.

Nutritional Information Per Serving:

Calories 284 | Fat 7.9g |Sodium 704mg | Carbs 6g | Fiber 3.6g | Sugar 6g | Protein 18g

Zucchini Noodle Bowl

Prep Time: 15 minutes.

Cook Time: 13 minutes.

Serves: 4

Ingredients:

- 2 small zucchinis
- ½ avocado
- ¼ cup olive oil
- 2 tbsp water
- 1-2 garlic cloves
- 2 sweet potatoes, peeled and diced
- 2 eggs
- 1-2 tbsp green onion for garnish
- Salt and black pepper to taste

Preparation:

1. Sauté sweet potatoes with 2 tbsp oil in a skillet until golden brown.
2. Pass the zucchini through the spiralizer and add the zucchini noodles to the skillet.
3. Sauté for 3 minutes then keep it aside.
4. Blend avocado mash with 2 tbsp oil and garlic in a blender.
5. Add this avocado cream to the noodles and mix well.
6. Top the noodles with the poached eggs and garnish with green onion, black pepper and salt.
7. Serve warm.

Serving Suggestion: Serve the zucchini bowl with crispy bacon on top.

Variation Tip: Top with chopped fresh herbs.

Nutritional Information Per Serving:

Calories 322 | Fat 12g |Sodium 202mg | Carbs 24.6g | Fiber 4g | Sugar 8g | Protein 17.3g

Oatmeal With Zucchini

Prep Time: 15 minutes.

Cook Time: 10 minutes.

Serves: 4

Ingredients:

- ¾ cup egg whites
- ¾ cup unsweetened vanilla almond milk
- 1 ½ tablespoon ground flaxseed
- ½ large banana, mashed
- ½ zucchini, grated
- ½ teaspoon cinnamon

Preparation:

1. Mash banana and zucchini in a suitable bowl.
2. Beat egg whites with almond milk in a saucepan and cook on medium heat.
3. Stir in flaxseed and cook until the mixture thickens.
4. Stir in banana mixture and cinnamon.
5. Garnish as desired and serve warm.

Serving Suggestion: Serve the oatmeal with yogurt.

Variation Tip: Add shredded coconut on top.

Nutritional Information Per Serving:

Calories 380 | Fat 19g |Sodium 318mg | Carbs 9g | Fiber 5g | Sugar 3g | Protein 26g

Grain Free Oatmeal

Prep Time: 15 minutes.

Cook Time: 0 minutes.

Serves: 4

Ingredients:

- ½ medium apple or 1 small apple
- 1 date
- 1 tbsp chia seeds
- 1 tbsp unsweetened coconut
- 1 tbsp slivered almonds
- almond butter for topping
- splash of Silk Cashew Milk

Preparation:

1. Blend apple with date, coconut, chia seeds and almonds in a food processor until grainy.
2. Serve the oatmeal with milk and almond butter in a bowl.
3. Serve.

Serving Suggestion: Serve the oatmeal with yogurt.

Variation Tip: Add shredded coconut on top.

Nutritional Information Per Serving:

Calories 404 | Fat 13g |Sodium 216mg | Carbs 7g | Fiber 3g | Sugar 4g | Protein 31g

Green Shakshuka

Prep Time: 15 minutes.

Cook Time: 23 minutes.

Serves: 5

Ingredients:

- 2 tbsp olive oil
- ½ medium onion, diced
- 4 garlic cloves, finely chopped
- 9 oz. brussels sprouts, shaved
- 1 zucchini, grated
- 1 tsp cumin
- ½ tsp salt
- ¼ tsp pepper
- 2 cups packed baby spinach
- 5 large eggs
- ¼ cup fresh cilantro, chopped
- 1 large avocado, for garnish

Preparation:

1. Sauté onion with oil in a sauté pan for 3 minutes.
2. Stir in garlic then sauté for 1 minute.
3. Add shaved Brussel sprouts and cook for 5 minutes.
4. Stir in zucchini and spices then cook for 1 minute.
5. Add spinach and cook for 3 minutes on low heat.
6. Make 5 wells in the mixture and crack 1 egg in each then cover.
7. Cook until the eggs are set then garnish with avocado slices and cilantro.
8. Serve.

Serving Suggestion: Serve the shakshuka with cucumber salad.

Variation Tip: Add broccoli to the meal.

Nutritional Information Per Serving:

Calories 348 | Fat 12g |Sodium 710mg | Carbs 4g | Fiber 5g | Sugar 3g | Protein 31g

Zucchini Sweet Potato Latkes

Prep Time: 15 minutes.

Cook Time: 6 minutes.

Serves: 4

Ingredients:

- 1 cup shredded zucchini
- 1 cup shredded sweet potato
- 1 egg, beaten
- 1 Tbsp coconut flour
- ½tsp garlic powder
- ¼ tsp ground cumin
- ½ tsp dried parsley
- Salt and black pepper to taste
- 1 Tbsp ghee or clarified butter
- 1 Tbsp EV olive oil

Preparation:

1. Beat egg in a bowl then add sweet potatoes and zucchini.
2. Mix coconut flour with spices and then add to the zucchini mixture.
3. Set a nonstick pan with ghee or olive oil on medium heat.
4. Add ¼ of the zucchini mixture in the skillet, flatten each and cook for 3 minutes per side.
5. Make more latkes with the remaining mixture in the same way.
6. Serve warm.

Serving Suggestion: Serve the latkes with yogurt dip and peas snaps.

Variation Tip: Add grilled zucchini to the platter as well.

Nutritional Information Per Serving:

Calories 375 | Fat 16g |Sodium 255mg | Carbs 4.1g | Fiber 1.2g | Sugar 5g | Protein 24.1g

Sweet Potatoes With Avocado Sauce

Prep Time: 15 minutes.

Cook Time: 20 minutes.

Serves: 3

Ingredients:

- 1 large sweet potato, cut into wedges
- 1 avocado, peeled and pitted
- 1 tablespoon olive oil
- Lemon or lime wedges
- Sesame seeds
- Crushed red pepper
- Sliced green onions
- Salt, pepper, and garlic powder to taste

Preparation:

1. Slice the sweet potato and mix with garlic powder, black pepper, salt and oil in a bowl.
2. Sauté the sweet potatoes in a skillet for 10 minutes per side.
3. Serve the potatoes with avocado, sesame seeds and rest of the ingredients.
4. Serve.

Serving Suggestion: Serve the potatoes with fried cauliflower rice.

Variation Tip: You can add dried herbs for seasoning as well.

Nutritional Information Per Serving:

Calories 373 | Fat 8g |Sodium 146mg | Carbs 8g | Fiber 5g | Sugar 1g | Protein 23g

Potato Shredded Pork Salad

Prep Time: 15 minutes.

Cook Time: 0 minutes.

Serves: 4

Ingredients:

- 2 tablespoons olive oil
- ½ lemon, juiced
- ¼ teaspoon paprika
- Salt, to taste
- Black pepper, to taste
- 3 medium baked potatoes, cooled and cut in 1-inch pieces
- 9 oz. meal prep slow-cooker pork
- 1 large seedless cucumber, cut in 1-inch pieces
- ½ large avocado
- 3 tablespoons fresh parsley

Preparation:

1. Mix pork, potatoes, black pepper, salt, lemon juice and oil in a bowl.
2. Divide this mixture in three bowls.
3. Serve.

Serving Suggestion: Serve the salad with cucumber dip.

Variation Tip: Drizzle dried herbs on top.

Nutritional Information Per Serving:

Calories 357 | Fat 12g |Sodium 48mg | Carbs 6g | Fiber 2g | Sugar 0g | Protein 24g

Salmon Asparagus Bundles

Prep Time: 15 minutes.

Cook Time: 23 minutes.

Serves: 6

Ingredients:

- 1 lb. asparagus spears
- 1 tbsp olive oil
- ¼ tsp salt
- ⅛tsp garlic powder
- ⅛ tsp paprika
- 1 pinch cayenne pepper
- 1 medium red bell pepper
- 4 oz smoked salmon

Preparation:

1. At 425 degrees F, preheat your oven.
2. Layer a baking sheet with foil.
3. Toss the asparagus spears with cayenne pepper, paprika, garlic powder, salt and oil in the baking sheet.
4. Cut the bell pepper in half and remove the seeds and ribs.
5. Add the peppers to the asparagus and roast for 10 minutes.
6. Stir and roast for 10 minutes then allow them to cool.
7. Slice the peppers and chop the asparagus.
8. Wrap bell pepper slices and asparagus pieces in a smoked salmon slice.
9. Secure the rolls in with a toothpick and make more rolls.
10. Place them in a baking sheet and broil them for 3 minutes.
11. Serve warm.

Serving Suggestion: Serve the bundles with roasted cauliflower mash.

Variation Tip: Add some paprika to the seasoning.

Nutritional Information Per Serving:

Calories 329 | Fat 5g |Sodium 510mg | Carbs 7g | Fiber 5g | Sugar 4g | Protein 21g

Meatball Egg Soup

Prep Time: 15 minutes.

Cook Time: 30 minutes.

Serves: 6

Ingredients:

Meatballs

- 1 lb. ground turkey
- 1 large shredded carrot
- 2 tablespoons fresh cilantro, chopped
- 1 red chili, chopped
- ¼ cup green onion, chopped
- 2 tablespoons fresh grated ginger
- 2 tablespoons coconut aminos
- ¼ teaspoon salt
- ½ teaspoon black pepper
- 1 egg
- 1 dash red pepper flakes

Soup

- 1 tablespoon sesame oil
- 1 tablespoon minced ginger
- 2 red chilies, deseeded and chopped
- 4 cups chicken stock
- 1 ½ cups water
- 2 tablespoons coconut aminos
- 1 teaspoon fish sauce
- 1 tablespoon lime juice
- 3 large eggs whisked
- ½ cup spring onions chopped
- 1 large carrot, cut into matchsticks
- 2 tablespoons cilantro, chopped
- Salt and black pepper to taste

Preparation:

1. At 400 degrees F, preheat your oven.
2. Mix all the turkey meatball ingredients in a bowl and make 2 inches meatballs.
3. Place these meatballs in a baking sheet and bake for 25 minutes.
4. Meanwhile, sauté ginger and chopped chili with sesame oil in a large pot for 2 minutes.
5. Stir in coconut aminos, water, stock, and fish sauce.
6. Beat the eggs in a suitable bowl then pour into the soup and cook while stirring.
7. Reduce its heat then add cilantro, carrot and spring onions.
8. Cook for 1 minute then add meatballs, black pepper and salt.
9. Garnish with cilantro and spring onions.
10. Serve warm.

Serving Suggestion: Serve the soup with warm bread.

Variation Tip: Add a pinch of sugar to season the soup mildly sweet.

Nutritional Information Per Serving:

Calories 382 | Fat 4g |Sodium 232mg | Carbs 4g | Fiber 1g | Sugar 0g | Protein 21g

Kale Salad With Sautéed Apples

Prep Time: 15 minutes.

Cook Time: 17 minutes.

Serves: 4

Ingredients:

- 1 large bunch kale, cut into thin ribbons
- zest of 1 lemon
- 2 tablespoons lemon juice
- 1 garlic clove, smashed and minced
- Sea salt to taste
- 3 tablespoons olive oil
- 1 shallot, peeled and sliced
- 4 apples, cored and cut into slices
- ½io cup raw pepitas, hulled

Preparation:

1. Toss kale with lemon juice, garlic, salt, and olive oil in a skillet.
2. Sauté the shallots with oil in a skillet for 10 minutes.
3. Stir in apples and cook for 5 minutes.
4. Add kale and rest of the ingredients then cook for 2 minutes.
5. Serve.

Serving Suggestion: Serve the salad with shrimp skewers on the side.

Variation Tip: Add lemon juice for a refreshing taste.

Nutritional Information Per Serving:

Calories 335 | Fat 25g |Sodium 122mg | Carbs 3g | Fiber 0.4g | Sugar 1g | Protein 33g

Curried Cauliflower Rice Kale Soup

Prep Time: 15 minutes.

Cook Time: 47 minutes.

Serves: 6

Ingredients:

- 5 cups of cauliflower florets
- 3 tbsp curry powder
- 1 tsp garlic powder
- ½ tsp cumin
- ½ tsp paprika
- ¼tsp sea salt
- 3 tbsp olive oil
- ¾ cup red onion, chopped
- 1 tsp garlic, minced
- 2 tsp olive oil

- 8 kale leaves, chopped
- 2 cups carrots, chopped
- 4 cups vegetable broth
- 1 cup almond milk
- ½ tsp red pepper
- ½ tsp black pepper

Preparation:

1. At 400 degrees F, preheat your oven.

2. Toss cauliflower florets with 3 tbsp oil, salt, paprika, cumin, garlic powder, and curry powder in a small bowl.

3. Spread these florets in a baking dish and roast for 22 minutes.

4. Grind the cauliflower in a food processor to get the rice.

5. Sauté garlic with 2 tbsp oil in a skillet for 5 minutes.

6. Stir in milk, broth, veggies, red chili pepper, black pepper and cauliflower rice.

7. Cook to a boil, then reduce its heat and cook for 20 minutes.

8. Serve warm.

Serving Suggestion: Serve the soup with fresh kale salad.

Variation Tip: Add shredded cheese to the soup.

Nutritional Information Per Serving:

Calories 440 | Fat 5g |Sodium 244mg | Carbs 6g | Fiber 1g | Sugar 1g | Protein 27g

Pulled Pork Lettuce Wraps With Avocado Aioli

Prep Time: 15 minutes.

Cook Time: 0 minutes.

Serves: 4

Ingredients:

- ½ avocado, peeled and pitted
- 2 tablespoons mayonnaise
- 1 lime, juiced
- 1 garlic clove, minced
- Salt and black pepper, to taste
- Water, for thinning

Lettuce wraps

- 1 head iceberg lettuce, broken into lettuce cups
- 2 cups chipotle pulled pork, warmed
- 1 avocado, sliced
- Lime wedges and cilantro, for garnishing

Preparation:

1. Mash avocado with mayo, black pepper, salt, lime juice and garlic in a bowl.
2. Top the lettuce cups with pork, and avocado mash.
3. Serve.

Serving Suggestion: Serve the wraps with parsley on top.

Variation Tip: Add lemon juice for good taste.

Nutritional Information Per Serving:

Calories 418 | Fat 22g |Sodium 350mg | Carbs 2.2g | Fiber 0.7g | Sugar 1g | Protein 24.3g

Roasted Chicken Salad

Prep Time: 15 minutes.

Cook Time: 0 minutes.

Serves: 4

Ingredients:

- 2 lb. chicken breast, cooked and cubed
- ½ cup carrot, shredded
- ¼ cup red onion, diced
- ½ cup roasted red pepper, chopped
- ¼ cup mayonnaise
- 1 tsp parsley, chopped
- 1 tsp garlic powder
- 1 tsp paprika
- Salt and black pepper to taste

Garlic mayonnaise

- 2 garlic cloves, roasted and chopped
- ¼ cup mayonnaise
- 1 tsp salt

Preparation:

1. Mix mayonnaise with salt, black pepper, paprika, and garlic powder in a bowl.
2. Stir in chicken, veggies and rest of the ingredients.
3. Mix well and serve.

Serving Suggestion: Serve the salad with sautéed broccoli.

Variation Tip: Drizzle paprika on top for more spice.

Nutritional Information Per Serving:

Calories 401 | Fat 7g |Sodium 269mg | Carbs 5g | Fiber 4g | Sugar 12g | Protein 26g

Muffins With Sweet Potato Topping

Prep Time: 15 minutes.
Cook Time: 37 minutes.
Serves: 6

Ingredients:

Meatloaf

- 1 ½ lb. ground beef
- 2 tsp. cooking oil
- 1 small onion, minced
- 3 garlic cloves, peeled and minced
- ½ cup barbecue sauce
- 1 tsp. dried thyme
- ½ tsp. salt
- ½ tsp. black pepper

Topping

- 2 sweet potatoes, peeled and cubed
- 1 tbsp. coconut oil
- ¼ tsp. salt

Preparation:

1. At 350 degrees F, preheat your oven.
2. Sauté onions with oil in a skillet for 5 minutes.
3. Stir in garlic and cook for 30 seconds.
4. Mix beef with the onion mixture, barbecue sauce, dried thyme, black pepper, and salt in a bowl.
5. Divide this meat mixture in a 12 cup muffin pan.
6. Bake the meat muffins for 20 minutes in the oven.
7. Add sweet potatoes to a pan with boiling water, cover and cook for 12 minutes then drain.
8. Peel and blend the sweet potatoes with coconut oil in a bowl.
9. Divide the potato mixture into of the meatloaves and garnish with barbecue sauce.
10. Serve warm.

Serving Suggestion: Serve the muffins with steaming potato rice.

Variation Tip: Add 1 teaspoon of hot sauce on top.

Nutritional Information Per Serving:

Calories 361 | Fat 16g |Sodium 189mg | Carbs 3g | Fiber 0.3g | Sugar 18.2g | Protein 33.3g

Sesame Chicken Tenders With Dressing

Prep Time: 11 minutes.

Cook Time: 17 minutes.

Serves: 2

Ingredients:

Chicken Tenders

- 1 pound chicken tenders
- ½ cup coconut aminos
- 2 tablespoons toasted sesame oil
- 2 tablespoons rice wine vinegar
- 2 tablespoons minced ginger root
- 4 garlic cloves, minced or grated
- 1 teaspoon garlic powder
- ½ teaspoon red pepper flakes
- ½ teaspoon white pepper
- 2 teaspoons sea salt
- 1 ½cups raw sesame seeds

Dressing

- ⅓ cup orange juice
- 2 tablespoon rice wine vinegar
- 2 garlic cloves, minced
- 2 teaspoons minced ginger root
- 2 teaspoons coconut aminos
- 2 teaspoons toasted sesame oil
- ½ teaspoon sea salt
- ⅔ cup olive oil

Salad

- 2 avocados, sliced
- 10- oz. spring mix greens
- 4 oranges, peeled and segments

Preparation:

1. Mix coconut aminos, white pepper, red pepper, garlic powder, garlic, ginger, rice wine vinegar, and sesame oil in a bowl.

2. Pour this mixture over the chicken in a bowl.

3. Mix well, cover and refrigerate for 4 hours.

4. At 425 degrees F, preheat your oven.

5. Toast sesame seeds in a skillet for 3 minutes.

6. Spread the sesame seeds in an 8x5 inches baking dish.

7. Coat the chicken with the sesame seeds and place it in the baking sheet and roast for 10 minutes.

8. Flip and continue to roast for 4 minutes.

9. Blend the dressing ingredients in a blender.

10. Toss the salad ingredients with the dressing in a salad bowl.

11. Top the salad with the chicken tenders.

12. Serve.

Serving Suggestion: Serve the salad with a glass of green smoothie.

Variation Tip: Add a drizzle of cheese on top.

Nutritional Information Per Serving:

Calories 445 | Fat 7.9g |Sodium 581mg | Carbs 4g | Fiber 2.6g | Sugar 0.1g | Protein 42.5g

Frittata

Prep Time: 15 minutes.

Cook Time: 22 minutes.

Serves: 4

Ingredients:

- 1 tablespoon ghee
- 1 cup cooked chicken
- 1 cup frozen broccoli
- 4 large pastured eggs
- 2 tablespoons full-fat coconut milk
- 1 teaspoon kosher salt
- Black pepper, to taste

Preparation:

1. At 350 degrees F, preheat your oven.
2. Sauté chicken with oil in a skillet for 2 minutes.
3. Stir in broccoli ten cook for 5 minutes.
4. Beat eggs with black pepper, salt, and coconut milk in a bowl.
5. Pour this mixture into the pan and bake for 15 minutes in the oven.
6. Slice and serve.

Serving Suggestion: Serve the frittata with bread and roasted veggies.

Variation Tip: Use toasted sesame seeds and herbs for garnishing.

Nutritional Information Per Serving:

Calories 384 | Fat 25g |Sodium 460mg | Carbs 6g | Fiber 0.4g | Sugar 2g | Protein 26g

Sweet Potato Chipotle Chili

Prep Time: 10 minutes.

Cook Time: 4 hrs. 2 minutes.

Serves: 4

Ingredients:

- 2 sweet potatoes, peeled and chopped
- 1 lb. ground lean pork
- 1 cup white onion, chopped
- 2 ½ cups broth
- 14 oz diced canned tomatoes
- 3 cup rice cauliflower
- 1 tsp minced garlic
- 2 chipotles with the adobo sauce, chopped
- 1 tsp cumin
- ½ tsp paprika
- ½ tsp chili powder
- ¼ tsp black pepper
- Sea salt to taste
- ½ cup bell peppers, chopped
- Fresh chopped Cilantro to garnish

Preparation:

1. Sauté meat with 1 tbsp water in a skillet until brown.
2. Stir in onion then sauté for 2 minutes then add to a slow cooker.
3. Add tomatoes and rest of the ingredients.
4. Cover and cook for 4 hours on a High heat.
5. Garnish and serve warm.

Serving Suggestion: Serve the chilli with white rice.

Variation Tip: Add some mixed herbs on top.

Nutritional Information Per Serving:

Calories 419 | Fat 13g |Sodium 432mg | Carbs 9.1g | Fiber 3g | Sugar 1g | Protein 33g

Salmon Cakes

Prep Time: 15 minutes.

Cook Time: 10 minutes.

Serves: 4

Ingredients:

Salmon Cakes:

- 1 lb. fresh Atlantic salmon side
- ¼ cup avocado, mashed
- ¼ cup cilantro, diced
- 1 ½ tsp yellow curry powder
- ½ tsp sea salt
- 4 tsp tapioca starch

Coating:

- ¼ cup tapioca starch
- 2 eggs
- ½ cup coconut flakes
- Coconut oil, melted, for brushing

Greens:

- 2 tsp coconut oil, melted
- 6 cups arugula and spinach mix, tightly packed
- 1 pinch sea salt

Preparation:

1. Blend salon with avocado, salt, curry powder, and cilantro in a food processor

2. Make 8 equal sized patties out of this mixture.

3. At 400 degrees F, preheat your Air Fryer.

4. Coat the patties with tapioca starch then dip them in the beaten egg and coat with coconut flakes.

5. Place the patties in the Air fryer basket and air fry for 10 minutes.

6. Flip the patties once cooked halfway through.

7. Toss the greens with oil and salt in a bowl.

8. Serve the patties with the greens.

Serving Suggestion: Serve the cakes with fresh herbs on top and a bowl of steamed rice.

Variation Tip: You can also coat the cakes crushed crackers.

Nutritional Information Per Serving:

Calories 388 | Fat 8g |Sodium 611mg | Carbs 8g | Fiber 0g | Sugar 4g | Protein 13g

Greek Salad

Prep Time: 10 minutes.
Cook Time: 0 minutes.
Serves: 4

Ingredients:

- Salad
- 3 heirloom tomatoes, diced
- 2 Roma tomatoes, diced
- 2 green bell peppers, diced
- 1 white onion, sliced
- 6 Persian cucumbers, sliced
- 2 tablespoons dried oregano
- 2 ½ tablespoons capers
- 1 cup kalamata olives pitted
- Black pepper to taste
- 1 block sheep's milk feta

Tzatziki Dressing

- 1 ½ cups raw cashews soaked
- 1 cup water
- 2 tablespoons fresh lemon juice
- 1 ½ cups cucumber grated
- ¾ teaspoon sea salt
- 5 garlic cloves
- 3 teaspoons white vinegar
- 2 tablespoons fresh dill chopped
- Sea salt to taste
- Black pepper to taste

Preparation:

1. Soak all the cashews in a bowl with hot water for 2 hours then drain.
2. Blend cashews with rest of sauce the ingredients except the dill and cucumber.
3. Mix the salad ingredients in a salad bowl.
4. Add the cucumber, and dill to the cashew dressing and mix well.
5. Pour the dressing into the salad then mix it well.
6. Serve.

Serving Suggestion: Serve the salad with mashed cauliflower.

Variation Tip: Add chopped sautéed bacon on top before serving.

Nutritional Information Per Serving:

Calories 429 | Fat 17g |Sodium 422mg | Carbs 5g | Fiber 0g | Sugar 1g | Protein 41g

Avocado Tuna Salad

Prep Time: 15 minutes.

Cook Time: 0 minutes.

Serves: 4

Ingredients:

- 1 avocado
- 1 lemon juiced, to taste
- 1 tablespoon onion, chopped
- 5 oz. cooked or canned wild tuna
- Sea salt to taste
- Black pepper to taste
- ½ bunch cilantro, torn into sprigs

Preparation:

1. Cut the avocado in half lengthwise then scoop out ¼ of the flesh from the center
2. Mash the avocado flesh in a bowl then add lemon juice, onion, black pepper, salt, and tuna.
3. Mix well then divide this mixture into the avocado shells.
4. Serve.

Serving Suggestion: Serve the salad with seafood skewers.

Variation Tip: Add sweet paprika for a tangy taste.

Nutritional Information Per Serving:

Calories 440 | Fat 14g |Sodium 220mg | Carbs 2g | Fiber 0.2g | Sugar 1g | Protein 37g

Almond Kale Salad With Sweet Potato

Prep Time: 10 minutes.

Cook Time: 0 minutes.

Serves: 4

Ingredients:

- 1 large apple, cored and chopped
- ½ lemon, juiced
- 4 cups kale
- 1 tablespoon almond butter
- Salt, to taste
- Black pepper, to taste
- 1 baked sweet potato, cut in ½-inch pieces
- 4 hard-boiled eggs, peeled and diced

Preparation:

1. Toss chopped apple with lemon juice in a bowl.
2. Toss kale with almond butter, black pepper, salt, sweet potato and apple in a bowl.
3. Serve.

Serving Suggestion: Serve the salad with a glass of protein smoothie.

Variation Tip: Toss the salad ingredients with some shredded cooked chicken.

Nutritional Information Per Serving:

Calories 352 | Fat 2.4g |Sodium 216mg | Carbs 6g | Fiber 2.3g | Sugar 1.2g | Protein 27g

Fried Cauliflower Rice

Prep Time: 15 minutes.

Cook Time: 15 minutes.

Serves: 4

Ingredients:

Rice

- 16 oz. cauliflower rice
- 1 large carrot, chopped
- 1 cup peas fresh
- ½ small onion, chopped
- 2 tablespoons sesame oil
- 2 large eggs, beaten

Sauce

- ¼ cup coconut aminos
- 3 tablespoons sesame oil
- 3 tablespoons date syrup
- 1 tablespoon arrowroot flour
- Frank's Hot sauce to taste

Preparation:

1. Blend date syrup and rest of the sauce ingredients in a blender.
2. Sauté cauliflower rice, onions, and carrots with 2 tbsp sesame oil in a skillet for 5 minutes.
3. Stir in peas and pour in beaten eggs.
4. Cover and cook until the eggs are set.
5. Garnish with sesame seeds and green onions.
6. Serve.

Serving Suggestion: Serve the rice with a green curry salmon.

Variation Tip: Add canned tomatoes to the rice.

Nutritional Information Per Serving:

Calories 301 | Fat 16g |Sodium 412mg | Carbs 3g | Fiber 0.2g | Sugar 1g | Protein 28.2g

Tuna Sushi Bowls

Prep Time: 15 minutes.

Cook Time: 15 minutes.

Serves: 4

Ingredients:

- 4 cups cooked rice
- Sushi vinegar, to taste
- 2 (5-oz.) cans tuna
- 3 tablespoons mayonnaise
- 1 teaspoon sriracha sauce
- ¾ cup frozen edamame
- 1 large carrot, julienned
- 1 avocado, peeled and pitted
- 1 cucumber, peeled and sliced
- Black sesame seeds
- ½ cup mayonnaise
- 1 tablespoon sriracha sauce
- 1 teaspoon honey

Preparation:

1. Mix the rice with 2 tbsp vinegar in a bowl.
2. Add sriracha sauce, mayonnaise and tuna in a bowl.
3. Top the rice with the tuna mixture, sesame seeds, avocado, carrots and edamame.
4. Mix the mayo ingredients in a bowl and pour over the rice bowl.
5. Enjoy.

Serving Suggestion: Serve the bowl with roasted veggies on the side.

Variation Tip: Add sweet paprika for more taste.

Nutritional Information Per Serving:

Calories 334 | Fat 16g |Sodium 462mg | Carbs 3g | Fiber 0.4g | Sugar 3g | Protein 35.3g

Chicken Bacon Asparagus Salad

Prep Time: 15 minutes.

Cook Time: 13 minutes.

Serves: 4

Ingredients:

- 2 cups asparagus, chopped
- 6 slices bacon
- 4 cups spinach, chopped
- 4 oz chicken breasts slices, cut into pieces
- ¼ cup sliced almonds

DRESSING

- ¼ cup olive oil
- 1 tablespoon red wine vinegar
- 1 teaspoon Dijon mustard
- ¼ teaspoon salt
- ¼ teaspoon black pepper

Preparation:

1. Boil the asparagus in a saucepan with water for 3 minutes then drain.
2. Sauté bacon strips in a skillet until brown.
3. Chop the cooked bacon and keep it aside.
4. Mix spinach with almonds, chicken, bacon and asparagus in a bowl.
5. Drizzle vinaigrette, black pepper and salt then mix well.
6. Serve.

Serving Suggestion: Serve the salad with sesame seeds and scallions on top.

Variation Tip: Add 1 tablespoon lime juice to the seasoning.

Nutritional Information Per Serving:

Calories 431 | Fat 20.1g |Sodium 364mg | Carbs 3g | Fiber 1g | Sugar 1.4g | Protein 15g

Skillet Roasted Chicken With Cabbage

Prep Time: 15 minutes.

Cook Time: 60 minutes.

Serves: 8

Ingredients:

- 1 green cabbage head, shredded
- 2 tsp salt
- 1 tbsp olive oil
- 1 (4 lb.) whole chicken, spatchcocked
- 3 tbsp taco seasoning rub

Preparation:

1. At 400 degrees F, preheat your oven.
2. Toss cabbage with oil and salt in a roasting pan.
3. Make space for the chicken and place it in the pan.
4. Rub the chicken with the taco seasoning and roast for 60 minutes in the oven.
5. Serve warm.

Serving Suggestion: Serve the chicken with cucumber salad.

Variation Tip: Add 1 tablespoon lime juice to the seasoning and marinate.

Nutritional Information Per Serving:

Calories 380 | Fat 8g |Sodium 339mg | Carbs 5.6g | Fiber 1g | Sugar 2g | Protein 21g

Curried Pumpkin Soup

Prep Time: 10 minutes.

Cook Time: 27 minutes.

Serves: 6

Ingredients:

- 2 ½ lbs. pumpkin, seeded, skinned and cubed
- 1 ½ lbs. butternut squash seeded, peeled and cubed
- 3 tbsp olive oil
- 2 onions, chopped
- 3 garlic cloves, chopped
- 2 tbsp curry powder
- ½ tsp grated nutmeg
- ½ tsp ground ginger
- ½ tsp red pepper
- 1 tsp salt
- ½ tsp black pepper
- 6 cups chicken stock
- ½ cup coconut milk
- Jalapeño, seeded, sliced
- Cilantro, to garnish
- Pumpkin seeds, to garnish

Preparation:

1. Sauté onions with oil in a large Dutch oven for 5 minutes.
2. Stir in garlic then sauté for 2 minutes.
3. Add pumpkin, squash, nutmeg, curry, ginger, salt, black pepper, red pepper and stock.
4. Cook this mixture to a boil then cook for 20 minutes on a simmer.
5. Puree the cooked soup with a hand blender.
6. Stir in black pepper, salt and coconut milk.
7. Garnish with pumpkin seeds, cilantro and jalapenos.
8. Serve warm.

Serving Suggestion: Serve the soup with roasted veggies and mashed cauliflower.

Variation Tip: Add dried herbs to the seasoning.

Nutritional Information Per Serving:

Calories 405 | Fat 20g |Sodium 941mg | Carbs 6.1g | Fiber 0.9g | Sugar 0.9g | Protein 45.2g

Sheet Pan Chicken Fajitas

Prep Time: 15 minutes.

Cook Time: 20 minutes.

Serves: 6

Ingredients:

- ¼ cup taco seasoning
- 1 tbsp olive oil
- 1 lime, juiced
- 2 lbs. boneless chicken breasts, cut into thin slices
- 1 red onion, sliced thin
- 1 red bell pepper, sliced thin
- 1 yellow bell pepper, sliced thin
- 1 green bell pepper, sliced thin
- Small flour tortillas, warmed
- Avocado, to garnish
- Cilantro, to garnish
- Salsa or hot sauce, to garnish

Preparation:

1. Mix taco seasoning with lime juice and olive oil in a large bowl.
2. Toss in bell peppers, red onion and chicken then mix well.
3. Cover and marinate the chicken for 1 hour.
4. At 375 degrees F, preheat your oven.
5. Spread the chicken and veggie mixture in a sheet pan and bake for 20 minutes.
6. Serve with warm tortillas, guacamole, salsa, sour cream avocado, and fresh cilantro.

Serving Suggestion: Serve the fajitas with avocado dip.

Variation Tip: Serve the fajitas on top of a lettuce bed.

Nutritional Information Per Serving:

Calories 376 | Fat 21g |Sodium 476mg | Carbs 2g | Fiber 3g | Sugar 4g | Protein 20g

Old Bay Shrimp And Sausage Sheet Pan

Prep Time: 15 minutes.

Cook Time: 17 minutes.

Serves: 6

Ingredients:

- 1 lb. raw, shrimp, peeled, deveined
- 1 lb. chicken sausage, cooked
- 1 lb. asparagus, trimmed and cut into 3" pieces
- 2 medium shallots, sliced into wedges
- 1 tbsp olive oil
- 1 tsp salt
- 2 tsp old bay seasoning
- 1 lemon
- Black pepper, to taste
- Lemon garlic aioli
- 1 cup olive oil
- 1 egg
- 1 garlic clove, smashed
- Zest of one lemon
- 1 tbsp lemon juice
- 1 tsp salt

Preparation:

1. Beat egg with salt, lemon juice and zest, garlic and oil in a blender.
2. At 400 degrees F, preheat your oven.
3. Toss asparagus, sausage and shallots with oil and ½ tsp salt in a baking sheet.
4. Roast for 10 minutes then toss in shrimp.
5. Add lemon juice, old bay seasoning, black pepper and salt on top.
6. Roast for 7 minutes.
7. Serve warm with the aioli.

Serving Suggestion: Serve the meal with grilled zucchini salad.

Variation Tip: Add crushed red pepper on top before serving.

Nutritional Information Per Serving:

Calories 380 | Fat 20g |Sodium 686mg | Carbs 3g | Fiber 1g | Sugar 1.2g | Protein 21g

Slow Cooker Chili

Prep Time: 10 minutes.
Cook Time: 8 hrs. 10 minutes.
Serves: 6

Ingredients:

- 2 lbs. chuck roast, diced
- 1 tbsp olive oil
- Salt and black pepper, to taste
- 1 lb. ground beef
- 1 large onion, diced
- 2 bell peppers, diced
- 3 cups zucchini, diced
- 1 cup mushrooms, chopped
- 5 garlic cloves, minced
- 1 (28 oz) can tomato sauce
- 1 (13 ½ oz) can fire roasted tomatoes, diced
- 1 (4 oz) can mild green chilies
- 2 cups beef stock
- 2 bay leaves
- 1 tbsp garlic powder, granulated
- ⅓ cup Chili powder
- 2 tbsp cumin
- Avocado, diced

- Cilantro, stems removed
- Jalapeños, diced
- Green onions, chopped

Preparation:

1. Rub the chuck roast with black pepper, salt and oil.
2. Sear the chuck roast in a skillet for 5 minutes per side.
3. Add the chuck roast and rest of the chili ingredients to a slow cooker.
4. Cover and cook the chilli for 8 hours on Low heat.
5. Shred the chuck roast and return to the chilli.
6. Garnish with green onions, cilantro, avocados and jalapenos.
7. Serve warm.

Serving Suggestion: Serve the chili with mashed cauliflower.

Variation Tip: Add crushed red pepper on top before serving.

Nutritional Information Per Serving:
Calories 391 | Fat 5g |Sodium 88mg | Carbs 3g | Fiber 0g | Sugar 0g | Protein 27g

Roasted Potatoes With Gremolata

Prep Time: 15 minutes.

Cook Time: 40 minutes.

Serves: 4

Ingredients:

- 2 ½ lbs. fingerling potatoes, cut in half
- ¼ cup olive oil
- 2 tsp sea salt

Gremolata

- ¾ cup chopped parsley
- ¼ cup fresh mint, minced
- 4 Garlic cloves, minced
- 2 tbsp Olive oil
- ½ tsp Salt
- 1 tbsp Lemon zest
- Juice from ½ lemon
- ¼ tsp red pepper flakes

Preparation:

1. Toss the potato with salt, and oil in a baking sheet.
2. At 400 degrees F, preheat your oven.
3. Roast the potatoes for 40 minutes in the oven.
4. Mix all the ingredients for gremolata in a bowl.
5. Serve the potatoes with the gremolata.

Serving Suggestion: Serve the potatoes a kale cucumber salad.

Variation Tip: Add crumbled bacon to the mixture.

Nutritional Information Per Serving:

Calories 325 | Fat 16g |Sodium 431mg | Carbs 2g | Fiber 1.2g | Sugar 4g | Protein 23g

Green Curry Salmon

Prep Time: 10 minutes.

Cook Time: 17 minutes.

Serves: 4

Ingredients:

- 4 (4 oz) Salmon fillets, skin removed
- ½tsp Salt
- ½ tsp black pepper
- 1 (13.5 oz) can coconut milk
- 1 tbsp green curry paste
- 1 tbsp lime juice
- 1 tsp grated ginger
- 1 tbsp fish sauce
- 2 tsp brown sugar
- 1 sweet onion, sliced
- 1 Red bell pepper, cored, sliced
- 1 green bell pepper, cored, sliced
- 4 green onions, chopped
- Fresh cilantro, to garnish

Preparation:

1. At 375 degrees F, preheat our oven.
2. Rub the salmon fillets with black pepper and salt.
3. Mix coconut milk with curry paste in a saucepan.
4. Stir in peppers, onions, fish sauce, brown sugar, ginger and lime juice then cook for 5 minutes.
5. Add the salmon in the curry and cook for 12 minutes.
6. Flip the salmon once cooked halfway through.
7. Garnish with the green onions and cilantro.
8. Serve warm with the rice.

Serving Suggestion: Serve the salmon with rice and mashed cauliflower.

Variation Tip: Add crushed red pepper on top before serving.

Nutritional Information Per Serving:

Calories 305 | Fat 25g |Sodium 532mg | Carbs 2.3g | Fiber 0.4g | Sugar 2g | Protein 18.3g

Vegetable Curry Soup

Prep Time: 15 minutes.

Cook Time: 29 minutes.

Serves: 6

Ingredients:

- 2 tbsp olive oil
- 1 onion, diced
- 1 large carrot, peeled and diced
- 2 stalks celery, diced
- 1 jalapeño seeded and minced
- 1 tsp fresh ginger, grated
- 2 large garlic cloves
- 2 tbsp yellow Indian curry powder
- 1 tbsp garam masala
- 4 cups vegetable stock
- ½ tsp salt
- 2 (12 oz.) cans coconut milk
- 2 tbsp cilantro, chopped
- 8 oz mushrooms, chopped
- 1 small eggplant, cut into 1" pieces
- 1 broccoli head, cut into small florets
- 1 red bell pepper, diced
- 1 small zucchini, diced

Preparation:

1. Sauté onions, jalapenos, carrots and celery with oil in a large pot for 1 minute.
2. Stir in ginger and garlic then cook for 2 minutes.
3. Add garam masala and curry the cook for 1 minute.
4. Stir in coconut milk, salt and rest of the ingredients then cook for 25 minutes on a simmer.
5. Garnish with cilantro and serve warm with flatbread.
6. Enjoy.

Serving Suggestion: Serve the soup with cauliflower casserole.

Variation Tip: Add crushed red pepper on top before serving.

Nutritional Information Per Serving:

Calories 425 | Fat 15g |Sodium 345mg | Carbs 2.3g | Fiber 1.4g | Sugar 3g | Protein 23.3g

Mango Salsa On Pan-Seared Salmon

Prep Time: 10 minutes.

Cook Time: 10 minutes.

Serves: 4

Ingredients:

Salsa:

- 2 cups diced ripe mango
- ½ cup red onion, diced
- 1 cup diced Hass avocado
- ¼ cup fresh cilantro, minced
- 2 tablespoons olive oil
- Black pepper, to taste
- 1 pinch of kosher salt
- ¼ teaspoon red pepper flakes
- Juice from 1 lime

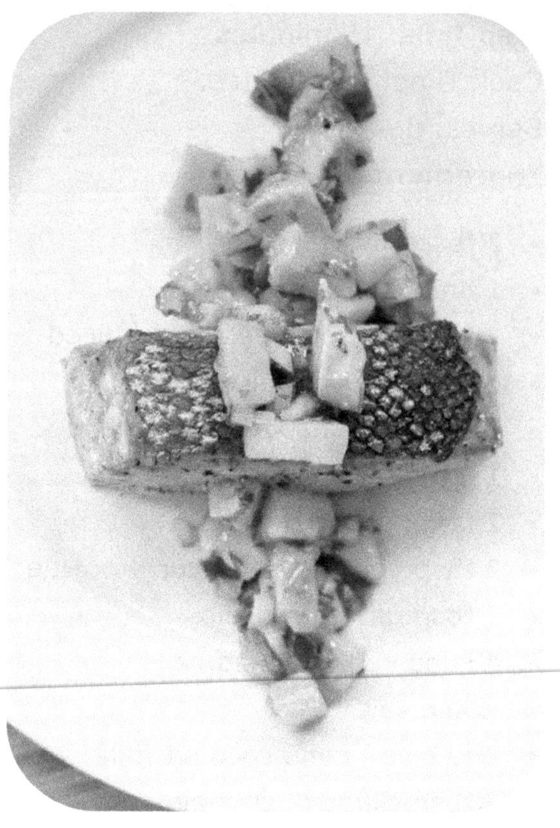

Salmon:

- 1½ pounds king salmon filet
- 2 tablespoons ghee
- Kosher salt, to taste
- Black pepper, to taste

Preparation:

1. Toss all the mango salsa ingredients in a suitable bowl and keep it refrigerated.
2. Season the salmon with black pepper and salt.
3. Sear the salmon in a skillet with ghee for 5 minutes per side.
4. Serve the salmon with mango salsa.

Serving Suggestion: Serve the salmon with boiled rice or grilled zucchini.

Variation Tip: Add crushed or sliced almonds to the serving.

Nutritional Information Per Serving:

Calories 361 | Fat 16g |Sodium 515mg | Carbs 29.3g | Fiber 0.1g | Sugar 18.2g | Protein 33.3g

Chicken Milanese With Ranch

Prep Time: 15 minutes.

Cook Time: 4 minutes.

Serves: 4

Ingredients:

Ranch:

- ½ cup mayo
- 3 tbsp plain almond milk
- 1 tbsp fresh lemon juice
- 2 tbsp fresh minced parsley
- 1 tsp fresh minced dill
- ¼ tsp onion powder
- ¼ tsp garlic powder
- ¼ tsp black pepper
- Sea salt to taste

Chicken:

- 1 ¼ lbs. boneless chicken breasts
- Salt and black pepper for sprinkling
- ¼ cup tapioca flour
- 1 cup blanched almond flour
- ¾ tsp garlic powder
- ¾ tsp onion powder
- 1 ½ tsp Italian seasoning
- ¼ tsp crushed red pepper
- ¼ tsp black pepper
- 1 ¼ tsp salt
- 2 eggs beaten with 2 tsp water
- ¼ cup olive oil

Preparation:

1. Mix all the ranch ingredients in a bowl.
2. Pound the chicken with mallet and slice each into cutlets.

3. Rub the chicken with black pepper and salt.

4. Mix tapioca flour, salt, black pepper, red pepper, Italian seasoning, onion powder, garlic powder and almond flour in a bowl.

5. Beat eggs with water in a bowl.

6. Dip the chicken in the egg mixture then coat with the flour mixture.

7. Sear the chicken cutlets for 2 minutes per side.

8. Serve the chicken with the ranch sauce, salad and rice.

Serving Suggestion: Serve this chicken with rice.

Variation Tip: Add crushed red pepper on top before serving.

Nutritional Information Per Serving:

Calories 425 | Fat 14g |Sodium 411mg | Carbs 24g | Fiber 0.3g | Sugar 1g | Protein 28.3g

Baked Fish Sticks With Tartar Sauce

Prep Time: 10 minutes.

Cook Time: 14 minutes.

Serves: 4

Ingredients:

Fish Sticks

- Olive oil, to grease
- 1 lb. cod fillets, cut into 2–2 ½inch pieces
- 2 whole eggs
- 1 cup almond flour
- 2 tbsp. coconut flour
- 1½ tsp. garlic powder
- 1½ tsp. onion powder
- 1 tsp. sweet or smoked paprika
- 1 tsp. salt
- ½ tsp. black pepper

tartar sauce:

- ½ cup mayonnaise
- 3 tbsp. dill pickles, chopped
- 2 tsp. fresh dill
- 1 tbsp. lemon juice
- ¼ tsp. garlic powder
- 1 pinch of black pepper
- 1 tsp. honey

Preparation:

1. Whisk all the tartar sauce ingredients in a suitable bowl.
2. At 425 degrees F, preheat your oven.
3. Layer a baking sheet with parchment paper and grease with cooking spray.
4. Beat eggs in a shallow bowl.
5. Mix flour with black pepper, salt, paprika, garlic and onion in a bowl.
6. Coat the fish sticks with the flour mixture, dip in the egg mixture then coat with the flour mixture.
7. Spread the fish sticks in the baking sheet then bake for 8 minutes.
8. Flip and bake for 6 minutes.
9. Serve the fish sticks with the tartar sauce.

Serving Suggestion: Serve the fish with butter sauce on top.

Variation Tip: Grill the veggies on the side to serve with the fish.

Nutritional Information Per Serving:

Calories 392 | Fat 16g |Sodium 466mg | Carbs 23.9g | Fiber 0.9g | Sugar 0.6g | Protein 48g

Curry Butternut Squash Noodles

Prep Time: 15 minutes.

Cook Time: 27 minutes.

Serves: 4

Ingredients:

- 2 tablespoons avocado oil, divided
- ½ inch piece fresh ginger, peeled and grated
- 2 garlic cloves, minced
- 1 pinch red pepper flakes
- 1 tablespoon green curry paste
- 1 teaspoon cumin
- 1 tablespoon green curry paste
- 2 cups full fat coconut milk
- 2 teaspoons lime juice, more to taste
- 1 teaspoon fish sauce
- 1 teaspoon coconut sugar
- ½ teaspoon sea salt, more to taste
- 1 yellow onion, thinly sliced
- 1 red pepper, thinly sliced
- 1 green pepper, thinly sliced
- 3 cups butternut squash noodles
- 1 cup fresh spinach
- 1 tablespoon scallions, sliced
- 1 tablespoon cilantro, for garnish

- 1 lime, sliced into wedges
- 1 red chili pepper, sliced thin
- 1 cup fresh spinach

Preparation:

1. Mix salt, coconut sugar, fish sauce, lime juice and coconut milk in a saucepan.
2. Cook this sauce to a boil then reduce its heat and cook for 15 minutes.
3. Sauté onions, peppers and a pinch of salt in a skillet for 5 minutes.
4. Add butternuts squash noodles then cook for 7 minutes.
5. Stir in spinach and coconut curry sauce.
6. Garnish with scallions, red chili peppers and cilantro.
7. Serve warm.

Serving Suggestion: Serve the noodles with sautéed vegetables.

Variation Tip: Use some lemon juice as well for seasoning.

Nutritional Information Per Serving:

Calories 309 | Fat 25g |Sodium 463mg | Carbs 19.9g | Fiber 0.3g | Sugar 0.3g | Protein 18g

Salmon With Zucchini Salad

Prep Time: 15 minutes.

Cook Time: 10 minutes.

Serves: 4

Ingredients:

- 4 pieces salmon skin on
- 3 cups baby spinach
- 4 small zucchinis sliced
- 1 large cucumber peeled, sliced and halved
- 4 radishes, sliced
- 2 tbsp avocado oil
- Dill for garnish
- Sea salt and black pepper, to taste

Preparation:

1. Toss the zucchini with radishes, cucumber and spinach in a bowl.

2. Sear salmon in a skillet with avocado oil on medium heat for 5 minutes per side.

3. Add the salad to a bowl and top it with the salmon on top.

4. Garnish with the dill and serve.

Serving Suggestion: Serve the salmon on top of the rice.

Variation Tip: Add paprika for more spice.

Nutritional Information Per Serving:

Calories 448 | Fat 13g |Sodium 353mg | Carbs 23g | Fiber 0.4g | Sugar 1g | Protein 29g

Chicken Alfredo With Spaghetti Squash

Prep Time: 10 minutes.

Cook Time: 40 minutes.

Serves: 4-6

Ingredients:

Cashew alfredo sauce:

- 1 ½ cups cashews
- 1 cup almond milk
- 3 garlic cloves
- 3 tbsp lemon juice
- 3 tbsp nutritional yeast
- 1 ¼ tsp fine sea salt
- 1 tsp dried basil optional

Spaghetti squash and chicken:

- 1 spaghetti squash
- Avocado oil
- Sea salt and black pepper, to taste
- 1 ½ lbs. boneless skinless chicken thighs
- ½ tsp dried oregano
- ½ tsp dried basil
- 1 tbsp avocado oil or ghee
- Fresh Basil for garnish

Preparation:

1. Blend cashew with rest of the ingredients in a blender until smooth.
2. Cook this mixture in a saucepan for 5 minutes until the mixture thickens.
3. At 400 degrees F, preheat your oven.
4. Layer a baking sheet with parchment paper.
5. Cut the spaghetti squash in half and scoop out the seeds.
6. Place the in the baking sheet and rub with black pepper, salt, and oil.
7. Roast the squash for 25 minutes in the oven use a fork to remove the scrape the shreds.
8. Rub chicken with black pepper, salt, basil and oregano.

9. Sear chicken with oil in a skillet over medium-high heat for 5 minutes per side then slice the chicken.

10. Add the squash shreds to a bowl and top them with the chicken.

11. Top the chicken with the alfredo sauce.

12. Garnish with basil and serve.

Serving Suggestion: Serve the meal with crispy onion rings on the side.

Variation Tip: Add crushed red pepper on top before serving.

Nutritional Information Per Serving:

Calories 376 | Fat 17g |Sodium 1127mg | Carbs 34g | Fiber 1g | Sugar 3g | Protein 29g

Butternut Squash And Apple Hash

Prep Time: 10 minutes.

Cook Time: 15 minutes.

Serves: 6

Ingredients:

- 1½ tbsp. coconut oil
- 1 medium onion, diced
- 1 butternut squash, peeled and cubed
- 1 medium apple, cored and diced
- 12 oz. ground turkey
- ½ tsp. dried sage
- ¼ tsp. dried thyme
- ¼ tsp. garlic powder
- ½ tsp. sea salt
- Pinch of nutmeg
- Red pepper flakes
- 3 cups kale, washed and torn

Preparation:

1. Mix ground turkey with nutmeg, salt, garlic powder, thyme, and sage in a bowl.
2. Sauté butternut squash and onion with oil in a skillet for 8 minutes.
3. Stir in diced apple and 3 tbsp water then cook for 5 minutes.
4. Add turkey mixture and remaining oil then sauté for 6 minutes.
5. Stir in kale, cover and cook for 2 minutes.
6. Adjust seasoning with black pepper and salt.
7. Serve warm.

Serving Suggestion: Serve the hash with poached eggs.

Variation Tip: Add almond butter to the hash for more taste.

Nutritional Information Per Serving:

Calories 345 | Fat 36g |Sodium 272mg | Carbs 41g | Fiber 0.2g | Sugar 0.1g | Protein 22.5g

Pumpkin Chili

Prep Time: 10 minutes.

Cook Time: 41 minutes.

Serves: 6

Ingredients:

- 1 ½ tablespoons avocado oil
- 2 pounds ground meat
- 1 large yellow onion diced
- 8 garlic cloves minced
- 2 green bell peppers diced
- 28 oz. fire roasted tomatoes
- 1 ½ tablespoons chili powder
- 1 ½ tablespoons cacao powder
- ½ teaspoon nutmeg
- ½ teaspoon paprika
- 1 ½ teaspoons cinnamon
- 1 ½ teaspoons cumin
- 1 ½ teaspoons sea salt
- ½ teaspoon black pepper
- 2 cups bone broth
- 15 oz. canned pumpkin
- Sea salt and black pepper to taste

Preparation:

1. Sauté ground meat with oil in a large soup for 5 minutes.
2. Stir in bell peppers, garlic and onion then sauté for 6 minutes.
3. Add spices, cacao powder, tomatoes and broth then deglaze the pan.
4. Stir in pumpkin, black pepper and salt then cook for 30 minutes on a simmer with occasional stirring.
5. Serve warm.

Serving Suggestion: Serve the chili with fresh greens and chili sauce on the side.

Variation Tip: Add lemon juice and lemon zest on top before cooking.

Nutritional Information Per Serving:

Calories 457 | Fat 19g |Sodium 557mg | Carbs 29g | Fiber 1.8g | Sugar 1.2g | Protein 32.5g

Lamb With Scallion Rice

Prep Time: 10 minutes.

Cook Time: 35 minutes.

Serves: 4

Ingredients:

Scallion Rice:

- 1 large head cauliflower
- 4 scallions, chopped
- 1 tablespoon olive oil
- ¾ teaspoon salt
- ½teaspoon black pepper

LAMB:

- 1 cup fresh cilantro, chopped
- 1 cup fresh mint, chopped
- 2 limes, juiced
- 1 tablespoon fish sauce
- 1 tablespoon coconut sugar
- ½ teaspoon black pepper
- ½medium jalapeno, chopped
- 1 ½ pounds ground lamb
- 2 garlic cloves, chopped
- ¼ cup cashews, chopped

Preparation:

1. At 425 degrees F, preheat your oven.
2. Grind all the cauliflower florets in a food processor to rice them.
3. Sauté cauliflower rice and rest of the veggies with oil in a skillet for 25 minutes.
4. Sauté lamb with rest of its ingredients in a skillet for 10 minutes until brown.
5. Serve the lamb with the cauliflower rice.
6. Enjoy.

Serving Suggestion: Serve the lamb with fried rice.

Variation Tip: Add some butter sauce on top.

Nutritional Information Per Serving:

Calories 321 | Fat 7.4g |Sodium 356mg | Carbs 29.3g | Fiber 2.4g | Sugar 5g | Protein 37.2g

Sweet Potato Falafel Bowl

Prep Time: 10 minutes.

Cook Time: 20 minutes.

Serves: 6

Ingredients:

Falafel

- 1 cup sweet potato minced
- 1 cup cauliflower rice
- ¼ white onion
- ¼ bunch fresh cilantro
- ¼ bunch fresh parsley
- ¼ cup almond flour
- ¾ medium garlic cloves
- 1 tablespoon ground cumin
- 1 large egg
- 1 tablespoon coconut flour
- ½ teaspoon sea salt
- ½ teaspoon turmeric
- olive oil for cooking

Sauce

- ¼ cup full fat canned coconut milk
- ¼ cup paleo mayonnaise
- ¼ green bell pepper, chopped
- 2 tablespoons fresh mint, chopped
- 2 tablespoons chives, chopped
- 2 tablespoons fresh oregano
- 1 large garlic clove, chopped
- lemon juice from ½ lemon
- Salt and black pepper to taste

Other

- 2 cups rainbow chard, chopped

- 2 cups arugula, chopped
- ½ cup clover sprouts
- 1 small orange bell pepper julienned
- 1 small red bell pepper julienned
- 2 portobello mushrooms grilled
- 2 rounds pineapple grilled
- 1 small apple shredded
- 1 cup strawberries
- ½ cup raspberries
- ½ cup blueberries
- ¼ cup almonds crushed
- ¼ cup pumpkin seeds

Preparation:

1. At 400 degrees F, preheat your oven.
2. Layer a baking sheet with parchment paper.
3. Blend all the falafel ingredients in a food processor.
4. Bake small falafel balls and place them in the baking sheet.
5. Drizzle oil on top and bake for 20 minutes.
6. Flip the falafel balls once cooked halfway through.
7. Meanwhile, blend all the sauce ingredients in a blender.
8. Toss all the salad ingredients in a bowl and top the salad with the falafel and the sauce.
9. Serve.

Serving Suggestion: Serve the bowl with sautéed green beans and mashed cauliflower.

Variation Tip: Drizzle cheese on top before serving.

Nutritional Information Per Serving:

Calories 395 | Fat 9.5g |Sodium 655mg | Carbs 34g | Fiber 0.4g | Sugar 0.4g | Protein 28.3g

Whole Grain Naan Bread

Prep Time: 10 minutes.

Cook Time: 8 minutes.

Serves: 8

Ingredients:

- 1 cup all-purpose flour
- 1 cup whole grain flour
- 2 teaspoons brown sugar
- 1 tablespoon baking powder
- 1 teaspoon nutritional yeast
- 1 ½teaspoons garlic powder
- ½ teaspoon sea salt
- ¼ teaspoon ground black pepper
- ⅓ cup warm milk
- ½ cup Greek yoghurt
- 1 ½ tablespoons coconut oil
- 1 teaspoon parmesan cheese for sprinkling
- cilantro, parsley for topping

Preparation:

1. Mix all the flours with baking powder, brown sugar, garlic powder, nutritional yeast, salt and pepper in a large bowl.

2. Make a hole in the center of this dry mixture and gradually pour in warm milk and yoghurt.

3. Mix the ingredients well together using a spatula.

4. Once combined, knead the prepared dough with floured hands for 5 minutes.

5. Cover the bowl with a plastic sheet and let it rest for 30 minutes.

6. Divide the dough into 8 equal balls.

7. Spread each ball into a round shape flatbread using a rolling pin.

8. Meanwhile, heat a large pan over medium heat.

9. Place the rolled naan in the pan and cook for 2 minutes per side until well cooked.

10. Serve.

Serving Suggestion: Serve the bread with chilli and mashed cauliflower.

Variation Tip: Add more herbs of your choice to the chilli.

Nutritional Information Per Serving:

Calories 337 | Fat 20g |Sodium 719mg | Carbs 21g | Fiber 0.9g | Sugar 1.4g | Protein 37.8g

Lime Avocado Mousse

Prep Time: 10 minutes.

Cook Time: 0 minutes.

Serves: 4

Ingredients:

- ½ cup canned full-fat coconut milk
- 1 cup cashews, soaked overnight
- ½ cup date syrup
- 2 avocados, peeled and pitted
- 4 limes, zested and juiced
- Pinch of sea salt

Preparation:

1. Blend cashews with rest of the ingredients in a blender until creamy.
2. Serve.

Serving Suggestion: Serve the mousse with a glass of green smoothie.

Variation Tip: Garnish with nuts and seeds.

Nutritional Information Per Serving:

Calories 301 | Fat 5g |Sodium 340mg | Carbs 17g | Fiber 1.2g | Sugar 1.3g | Protein 15.3g

Chia Pudding

Prep Time: 10 minutes.

Cook Time: 0 minutes.

Serves: 1

Ingredients:

- 2 tablespoon chia seeds
- ½ cup almond milk
- 1 teaspoon honey
- Strawberries for topping

Preparation:

1. Add chia seeds, almond milk, and honey in a mason jar.
2. Refrigerate overnight then garnish with berries.
3. Serve.

Serving Suggestion: Serve the pudding with a glass of avocado smoothie

Variation Tip: Garnish with nuts and seeds.

Nutritional Information Per Serving:

Calories 248 | Fat 23g |Sodium 350mg | Carbs 18g | Fiber 6.3g | Sugar 1g | Protein 40.3g

Blueberry Cobbler

Prep Time: 15 minutes.

Cook Time: 25 minutes.

Serves: 4

Ingredients:

- 2 pints fresh blueberries
- Juice and zest of 1 lemon
- 4 tbsp tapioca flour
- ¾ cup almond flour
- 1 tsp baking powder
- ¼ tsp salt
- ¼ cup date syrup
- ¼ cup coconut oil
- 2 tbsp coconut milk

Preparation:

1. At 375 degrees F, preheat your oven.
2. Toss blueberries with 2 tbsp tapioca flour, lemon juice and zest in a bowl.
3. Divide this mixture into two small pie plates.
4. Toss coconut milk, coconut oil, date syrup, baking powder, almond flour and 2 tbsp tapioca flour in a bowl.
5. Divide this mixture on top of the berry mixture and bake for 25 minutes.
6. Serve.

Serving Suggestion: Serve the cobbler with a glass of a protein smoothie

Variation Tip: Garnish with nuts and seeds.

Nutritional Information Per Serving:

Calories 405 | Fat 22.7g |Sodium 227mg | Carbs 31g | Fiber 1.4g | Sugar 0.9g | Protein 45.2g

Chocolate Pudding Cakes

Prep Time: 20 minutes.

Cook Time: 8 minutes.

Serves: 6

Ingredients:

Batter:

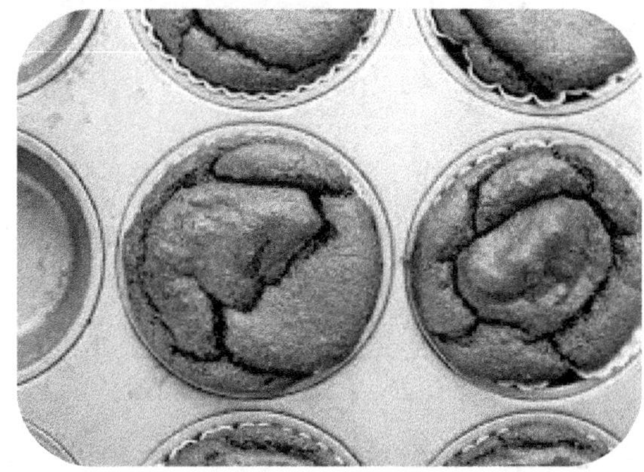

- ¾ cup almond meal
- ⅓ cup full-fat coconut milk
- ¼ cup raw cacao powder
- 1 egg
- 3 tbsp coconut oil
- 3 tbsp date syrup
- ½ tsp vanilla extract
- ½ tsp apple cider vinegar
- ¼ tsp sea salt

Sauce:

- ¾ cup hot water
- 2 tbsp date syrup
- ¼ cup raw cacao powder

Preparation:

1. Blend all the batter ingredients in a food processor.
2. Divide this batter in 4 ramekins.
3. Mix date syrup, hot water and cacao powder in a bowl then pour over the batter
4. Set a rack in the Instant Pot and pour in 1 cup water.
5. Place the ramekins on the rack, seal the pressure lid and cook for 8 minutes on High pressure.
6. Once done, release the pressure the completely then remove the lid.
7. Allow the cakes to cool and serve.

Serving Suggestion: Serve the cakes with a glass of avocado smoothie

Variation Tip: Garnish with nuts and seeds.

Nutritional Information Per Serving:

Calories 132 | Fat 10g |Sodium 994mg | Carbs 34g | Fiber 0.4g | Sugar 3g | Protein 8g

Date Squares

Prep Time: 15 minutes.

Cook Time: 41 minutes.

Serves: 4

Ingredients:

Filling:

- 1 orange, zested and juiced
- 1 pound pitted dates
- 1 cup water
- ¼ tsp salt

Crust and topping:

- 2 cups almond meal
- 1 cup unsweetened coconut flakes
- ¼ tsp sea salt
- ½ cup 2 tbsp coconut oil

Preparation:

1. At 350 degrees F, preheat your oven.
2. Layer an 8 inch squash pan with parchment paper.
3. Mix orange juice, salt, water, zest and dates in a small saucepan.
4. Cook for 6 minutes then blend until smooth.
5. Mix almond meal with coconut oil, sea salt, and coconut flakes in a bowl.
6. Spread and press ½ of the crust mixture in the pan then bake for 10 minutes.
7. Allow the crust to cool then add the date mixture.
8. Add the remaining crust mixture on top.
9. Bake for 25 minutes in the oven.
10. Slice the layers into squares.
11. Serve.

Serving Suggestion: Serve the date square with a glass of green smoothie

Variation Tip: Garnish with nuts and seeds.

Nutritional Information Per Serving:

Calories 82 | Fat 6g |Sodium 620mg | Carbs 25g | Fiber 2.4g | Sugar 1.2g | Protein 12g

Sautéed Apples With Caramel Drizzle

Prep Time: 10 minutes.

Cook Time: 5 minutes.

Serves: 4

Ingredients:

- 1 tbsp coconut oil
- 2 apples, peeled and sliced
- 1 tsp ground cinnamon
- ½ cup coconut cream
- ¼ cup date syrup
- ¼ tsp kosher salt

Preparation:

1. Sauté apples with cinnamon and coconut oil in a skillet for 5 minutes.
2. Blend coconut cream with salt and date syrup in a blender.
3. Serve the cream with apples on top.
4. Enjoy.

Serving Suggestion: Serve the apples with a glass of avocado smoothie

Variation Tip: Garnish with nuts and seeds.

Nutritional Information Per Serving:

Calories 449 | Fat 31g |Sodium 723mg | Carbs 22g | Fiber 2.5g | Sugar 2g | Protein 26g

Chocolate Coconut Pudding

Prep Time: 10 minutes.

Cook Time: 8 minutes.

Serves: 4

Ingredients:

- 1 ½ cups coconut cream
- ¼ cup raw cacao powder
- 3 tbsp date syrup
- 1 tsp vanilla extract
- ¼ tsp sea salt
- ¼ tsp espresso powder

Preparation:

1. Heat coconut cream in a saucepan then add cacao powder and date syrup
2. Cover and cook for 8 minutes until the mixture thickens.
3. Remove from the heat then add espresso powder, sea salt and vanilla extract.
4. Allow the pudding to cool and refrigerate for 1 hour.
5. Serve.

Serving Suggestion: Serve the pudding with a glass of avocado smoothie

Variation Tip: Garnish with nuts and seeds.

Nutritional Information Per Serving:

Calories 324 | Fat 1g |Sodium 236mg | Carbs 32g | Fiber 0.3g | Sugar 0.1g | Protein 1g

Instant Pot Lemon Cake

Prep Time: 10 minutes.

Cook Time: 41 minutes.

Serves: 6

Ingredients:

- 1 cup almond flour
- ½ cup tapioca flour
- ½ cup coconut flour
- 1 ½ tsp baking soda
- ½ tsp salt
- 3 eggs
- Zest and juice of 3 lemons
- ½ cup date syrup
- ½ cup canned coconut milk
- ½ cup melted coconut oil
- 1 teaspoon vanilla extract

Preparation:

1. Blend almond flour and rest of the ingredient in a food processor until smooth.
2. Spread this mixture in a 7 inch baking pan greased with cooking spray.
3. Set a rack in an Instant Pot and pour in 1 cup water.
4. Place the baking pan on the rack then seal the lid.
5. Cook on High pressure for 35 minutes.
6. Once done, release the pressure completely then remove the lid.
7. Allow the cake to cool then slice.
8. Serve.

Serving Suggestion: Serve the baked cake with a glass of green smoothie

Variation Tip: Garnish with frosting, nuts and seeds.

Nutritional Information Per Serving:

Calories 110 | Fat 6g |Sodium 220mg | Carbs 32g | Fiber 2.4g | Sugar 1.2g | Protein 12g

Banana Coconut Ice Cream

Prep Time: 15 minutes.

Cook Time: 20 minutes.

Serves: 4

Ingredients:

- 4 medium bananas
- 3 tbsp melted coconut oil
- 6 tbsp date syrup
- 1 (13 1/2-oz.) can full-fat coconut milk
- ¾ cup almonds, sliced

Preparation:

1. At 375 degrees F, preheat your oven.
2. Layer a baking sheet with parchment paper.
3. Place the banana slices in a baking sheet.
4. Drizzle date syrup and coconut oil on top and roast for 20 minutes.
5. Blend the roasted bananas with rest of the ingredients in a blender until smooth.
6. Add this mixture to a bowl, cover and refrigerate overnight.
7. Garnish with almonds.
8. Serve.

Serving Suggestion: Serve the ice cream with muffins.

Variation Tip: Garnish with nuts and seeds.

Nutritional Information Per Serving:

Calories 256 | Fat 4g |Sodium 634mg | Carbs 33g | Fiber 1.4g | Sugar 1g | Protein 3g

Fudgy Brownies

Prep Time: 10 minutes.

Cook Time: 22 minutes.

Serves: 6

Ingredients:

- Cooking spray
- ¾ cup unsweetened cocoa powder
- ½ cup almond flour
- 1 tsp. baking soda
- ½ tsp. kosher salt
- ½cup almond butter
- ½ cup coconut sugar
- ⅓ cup honey
- ¼ cup olive oil
- 2 large eggs
- 1 tsp. pure vanilla extract
- Sea salt, for sprinkling

Preparation:

1. At 350 degrees F, preheat your oven.
2. Layer an 8x8 inch baking pan with parchment paper and grease with a cooking spray.
3. Mix almond flour with salt, baking soda and coconut powder.
4. Beat almond butter and other ingredients in a bowl.
5. Pour this mixture into the flour mixture then mix well until smooth.
6. Spread this batter in the baking pan and bake for 22 minutes.
7. Allow the cake to cool then slice.
8. Serve.

Serving Suggestion: Serve the brownies with a glass of avocado smoothie

Variation Tip: Garnish with nuts and seeds.

Nutritional Information Per Serving:

Calories 338 | Fat 7g |Sodium 316mg | Carbs 24g | Fiber 0.3g | Sugar 0.3g | Protein 3g

Granola

Prep Time: 10 minutes.

Cook Time: 23 minutes.

Serves: 6

Ingredients:

- 1 cup almonds
- 1 cup pecans
- 1 cup dried cranberries
- ½ cup pumpkin seeds
- ½ cup unsweetened coconut flakes
- ¼ cup flax seeds
- ¼ cup sunflower seeds
- ¼ cup sesame seeds
- 1 tsp. kosher salt
- 1 tsp. ground cinnamon
- ½ tsp. ground nutmeg
- 3 tbsp. melted coconut oil
- ¼ cup honey
- 1 tsp. vanilla extract

Preparation:

1. At 350 degrees F, preheat your oven.
2. Grease a baking sheet with cooking spray.
3. Mix pecans, cranberries and rest of the ingredients in a bowl.
4. Stir in vanilla, honey, and oil then spread this mixture in the baking sheet.
5. Bake the granola for 23 minutes in the oven.
6. Serve.

Serving Suggestion: Serve the granola with zucchini chips.

Variation Tip: Add chopped peanuts as well.

Nutritional Information Per Serving:

Calories 185 | Fat 8g |Sodium 146mg | Carbs 5g | Fiber 0.1g | Sugar 0.4g | Protein 1g

Chicken Stuffed Avocados

Prep Time: 15 minutes.

Cook Time: 0 minutes.

Serves: 6

Ingredients:

- 3 avocados, halved and pits removed
- ½ Juice of 1/2 lemon
- 2 c. cooked and shredded chicken
- 2 large tomatoes, diced
- ¼ red onion, finely chopped
- 1 tbsp. olive oil
- ¼ tsp. red pepper flakes
- Kosher salt, to taste
- Freshly ground black pepper, to taste
- Balsamic glaze, for garnish
- Thinly sliced basil, for garnish

Preparation:

1. Cut the avocados in half and drizzle lemon juice on top.
2. Mix chicken with rest of the ingredients in a bowl.
3. Divide this mixture in the avocado halves.
4. Serve.

Serving Suggestion: Serve the avocados with lemon wedges.

Variation Tip: Add roasted asparagus on the side.

Nutritional Information Per Serving:

Calories 293 | Fat 3g |Sodium 510mg | Carbs 12g | Fiber 3g | Sugar 4g | Protein 4g

California Sushi Bites

Prep Time: 15 minutes.

Cook Time: 0 minutes.

Serves: 4

Ingredients:

- 1 avocado
- 1 Juice of 1 lemon
- 1 large cucumber, sliced into ¼" coins
- 8 oz. lump crabmeat
- ⅓ cup mayonnaise
- 2 tsp. Sriracha
- 3 green onions, sliced
- Sesame seeds, for garnish
- Soy sauce for serving

Preparation:

1. Toss avocado slices with lemon juice.
2. Top each cucumber slice with avocado, black pepper and salt.
3. Mix crabmeat with lemon juice, black pepper, salt, green onions, sriracha, and mayonnaise in a bowl.
4. Top each cucumber slice with the crab mixture and garnish with sesame seeds.
5. Serve.

Serving Suggestion: Serve the bites with fresh herbs on top.

Variation Tip: Add a drizzle of red pepper flakes and parmesan on top.

Nutritional Information Per Serving:

Calories 351 | Fat 19g |Sodium 412mg | Carbs 13g | Fiber 0.3g | Sugar 1g | Protein 23g

Brussels Sprout Chips

Prep Time: 15 minutes.

Cook Time: 12 minutes.

Serves: 6

Ingredients:

- 1 lb. Brussels sprouts, thinly sliced
- 2 tbsp. olive oil
- Kosher salt, to taste
- Black pepper, to taste
- ¼ cup finely grated Parmesan

Preparation:

1. At 400 degrees F, preheat your oven.
2. Toss brussels sprouts with oil, black pepper and salt in a baking sheet.
3. Drizzle parmesan on top and roast the Brussel sprouts for 12 minutes in the oven.
4. Serve.

Serving Suggestion: Serve the chips with a drizzle of parmesan on top.

Variation Tip: Add shredded coconut to the chips.

Nutritional Information Per Serving:

Calories 136 | Fat 20g |Sodium 249mg | Carbs 4g | Fiber 2g | Sugar 3g | Protein 4g

Guacamole

Prep Time: 10 minutes.

Cook Time: 0 minutes.

Serves: 6

Ingredients:

- 3 avocados, pitted
- Juice of 2 limes
- ¼cup freshly chopped cilantro
- ½ small white onion, chopped
- 1 small jalapeño, seeded, minced
- ½ tsp. kosher salt

Preparation:

1. Mash avocados in a bowl and stir in rest of the ingredients.
2. Mix well and serve.

Serving Suggestion: Serve the guacamole with Brussel sprout chips.

Variation Tip: Add a drizzle of sesame seeds and oil.

Nutritional Information Per Serving:

Calories 161 | Fat 10g |Sodium 218mg | Carbs 6g | Fiber 10g | Sugar 30g | Protein 14g

Buffalo Roasted Cauliflower

Prep Time: 10 minutes.

Cook Time: 25 minutes.

Serves: 2

Ingredients:

- 1 head cauliflower, cut into florets
- ¼ cup buffalo sauce

Preparation:

1. At 375 degrees F, preheat your oven.
2. Toss cauliflower florets with buffalo sauce in a bowl.
3. Spread the florets in a baking sheet and roast for 25 minutes in the oven.
4. Serve.

Serving Suggestion: Serve the cauliflower with boiled cauliflower rice.

Variation Tip: Top the cauliflower with feta cheese before serving.

Nutritional Information Per Serving:

Calories 341 | Fat 24g |Sodium 547mg | Carbs 6.4g | Fiber 1.2g | Sugar 1g | Protein 10.3g

Cucumber Sushi

Prep Time: 10 minutes.

Cook Time: 0 minutes.

Serves: 6

Ingredients:

Sushi

- 2 medium cucumbers
- ¼ avocado, sliced
- ½ red bell pepper, sliced
- ½ yellow bell pepper, sliced
- 2 small carrots, sliced

Dipping Sauce

- ⅓ cup mayonnaise
- 1 tbsp. sriracha
- 1 tsp. soy sauce

Preparation:

1. Mash avocado in a bowl and add rest of the veggies then mix well.
2. Use a small scoop or spoon to remove the seeds from the cucumber and make it hollow.
3. Stuff the cucumber with the avocado mixture then slices the cucumber into thick slices.
4. Mix the dipping sauce ingredients in a bowl.
5. Serve the cucumber slices with the sauce.

Serving Suggestion: Serve the sushi with butter sauce and bacon on top.

Variation Tip: Add boiled green beans on the side.

Nutritional Information Per Serving:

Calories 378 | Fat 3.8g |Sodium 620mg | Carbs 3.3g | Fiber 2.4g | Sugar 1.2g | Protein 5.4g

Healthy Cereal

Prep Time: 15 minutes.

Cook Time: 25 minutes.

Serves: 6

Ingredients:

- Cooking spray
- 1 cup almonds, chopped
- 1 cup walnuts, chopped
- 1 cup unsweetened coconut flakes
- ¼ cup sesame seeds
- 2 tbsp. flax seeds
- 2 tbsp. chia seeds
- ½ tsp. ground clove
- 1 ½ tsp. ground cinnamon
- 1 tsp. pure vanilla extract
- ½ tsp. kosher salt
- 1 large egg white
- ¼ cup melted coconut oil

Preparation:

1. At 350 degrees F, preheat your oven.
2. Grease a baking sheet with cooking spray.
3. Toss almonds with rest of the ingredients in a bowl.
4. Spread this mixture in the baking sheet and bake for 25 minutes.
5. Serve.

Serving Suggestion: Serve the cereal with milk

Variation Tip: Add chopped nuts on top.

Nutritional Information Per Serving:

Calories 391 | Fat 2.2g |Sodium 276mg | Carbs 27g | Fiber 0.9g | Sugar 1.4g | Protein 8.8g

Zucchini Sushi

Prep Time: 10 minutes.

Cook Time: 0 minutes.

Serves: 6

Ingredients:

- 2 medium zucchinis, peeled and cut into strips
- 4 oz. cream cheese, softened
- 1 tsp. Sriracha hot sauce
- 1 tsp. lime juice
- 1 cup lump crab meat
- ½ carrot, cut into thin matchsticks
- ½ avocado, diced
- ½ cucumber, cut into thin matchsticks
- 1 tsp. toasted sesame seeds

Preparation:

1. Cut the zucchini into thin slices and pat them dry.
2. Mix cream cheese, lime juice and Sriracha in a bowl.
3. Place 2 zucchini slices horizontally and add a thin layer of cream cheese on top.
4. Add a teaspoon of crab, cucumber, avocado and carrot on top.
5. Roll the zucchini slices and make more rolls with remaining ingredients.
6. Garnish with sesame seeds.
7. Enjoy.

Serving Suggestion: Serve the sushi with mashed cauliflower.

Variation Tip: Add crispy sweet potatoes on the side.

Nutritional Information Per Serving's

Calories 304 | Fat 31g |Sodium 834mg | Carbs 4.4g | Fiber 0.2g | Sugar 0.3g | Protein 4.6g

Tuna Salad Pickle Boats

Prep Time: 10 minutes.

Cook Time: 0 minutes.

Serves: 12

Ingredients:

- 2 (5-oz.) cans tuna, drained
- ¼ cup mayonnaise
- 1 tbsp. Dijon mustard
- 2 stalks celery, finely chopped
- Juice of ½ a lemon
- 1 tbsp. chopped dill
- kosher salt, to taste
- Black pepper, to taste
- 6 dill pickles, halved
- Paprika, for garnish

Preparation:

1. Cut the pickles in half and remove the seeds from the center.
2. Mix tuna, mayo and rest of the ingredients in a bowl.
3. Divide the tuna mixture in the pickle halves.
4. Garnish with paprika.
5. Serve.

Serving Suggestion: Serve the boated with roasted mushrooms.

Variation Tip: Add lemon zest and lemon juice on top for better taste.

Nutritional Information Per Serving:

Calories 324 | Fat 5g |Sodium 432mg | Carbs 3.1g | Fiber 0.3g | Sugar 1g | Protein 5.7g

Spicy Guacamole Sauce

Prep Time: 5 minutes.

Cook Time: 0 minutes.

Serves: 8

Ingredients:

- ¼ cup cilantro, packed
- ½ avocado
- ¼ medium white onion, chopped
- 1 small garlic clove, chopped
- Juice from ½ lime
- ½ jalapeño
- ¼ teaspoon sea salt

Preparation:

1. Mash avocado in a bowl then add cilantro and other ingredients.
2. Mix well and serve.

Serving Suggestion: Serve the sauce with zucchini noodles.

Variation Tip: Add green beans around before serving.

Nutritional Information Per Serving:

Calories 85 | Fat 15.7g |Sodium 124mg | Carbs 7g | Fiber 0.1g | Sugar 0.3g | Protein 4.9g

Jalapeno Cilantro Chimichurri

Prep Time: 5 minutes.

Cook Time: 0 minutes.

Serves: 8

Ingredients:

- 1 ½ cups cilantro
- ½ cup olive oil
- ¼ cup red wine vinegar
- 1 large garlic clove, minced
- 1 teaspoon oregano
- ½ jalapeno, deseeded
- ½ teaspoon sea salt

Preparation:

1. Blend cilantro, oregano and rest of the ingredients in a blender.
2. Serve.

Serving Suggestion: Serve the sauces with roasted veggies.

Variation Tip: Add crushed cashews to the sauce.

Nutritional Information Per Serving:

Calories 53 | Fat 1g |Sodium 8mg | Carbs 6.6g | Fiber 0.8g | Sugar 56g | Protein 1g

Creamy Bacon Mushroom Sauce

Prep Time: 15 minutes.

Cook Time: 11 minutes.

Serves: 12

Ingredients:

- 6 cremini mushrooms
- 2 slices of bacon
- 1 small shallot
- 1 teaspoon fresh thyme
- ⅓ cup raw cashews
- ½ cup chicken stock
- ¼ teaspoon salt and black pepper

Preparation:

1. Sauté bacon in a skillet until brown.
2. Stir in mushrooms then sauté for 10 minutes.
3. Add shallot then sauté for 1 minute.
4. Blend the mixture with rest of the ingredients in a blender until smooth.
5. Serve.

Serving Suggestion: Serve the sauce with spaghetti squash.

Variation Tip: Add crushed pecans to the sauce.

Nutritional Information Per Serving:

Calories 95 | Fat 3g |Sodium 355mg | Carbs 7.7g | Fiber 1g | Sugar 25g | Protein 1g

Mustard Sauce

Prep Time: 5 minutes.

Cook Time: 0 minutes.

Serves: 8

Ingredients:

- 1 cup pitted dates, soaked
- ⅓ cup Dijon mustard
- ¼ cup avocado oil
- ¼ cup water
- ¼ teaspoon salt

Preparation:

1. Blend dates, mustard and rest of the ingredients in a blender.
2. Serve.

Serving Suggestion: Serve the sauce with kale salad.

Variation Tip: Add crushed walnuts or pecans to the sauce.

Nutritional Information Per Serving:

Calories 103 | Fat 8.9g |Sodium 340mg | Carbs 7.2g | Fiber 1.2g | Sugar 11.3g | Protein 5.3g

Cauliflower Cheese Sauce

Prep Time: 15 minutes.

Cook Time: 20 minutes.

Serves: 8

Ingredients:

- ½ medium cauliflower, minced
- 2 tablespoons hot sauce
- 3 tablespoons nutritional yeast
- ¼ teaspoon salt
- ¼ cup raw cashews
- ½ cup water

Preparation:

1. At 375 degrees F, preheat your oven.
2. Spread the cauliflower florets in a baking sheet then roast for 20 minutes,
3. Blend the cauliflower florets in a blender with rest of the ingredients until smooth.
4. Serve.

Serving Suggestion: Serve the sauce with crispy crackers.

Variation Tip: Add chopped nuts to the sauce.

Nutritional Information Per Serving:

Calories 148 | Fat 16g |Sodium 95mg | Carbs 8.4g | Fiber 0.3g | Sugar 10g | Protein 14.1g

Almond Lime Satay

Prep Time: 5 minutes.

Cook Time: 0 minutes.

Serves: 8

Ingredients:

- ½ cup coconut milk
- 6 tablespoons roasted almond butter
- 1 tablespoon coco aminos
- 1 small garlic clove
- Juice from 1 lime
- ¼ teaspoon salt

Preparation:

1. Blend coconut milk with butter and rest of the ingredients in a blender.
2. Serve.

Serving Suggestion: Serve the satay with roasted kebabs,

Variation Tip: Add crushed walnuts or pecans to the satay.

Nutritional Information Per Serving:

Calories 98 | Fat 14g |Sodium 272mg | Carbs 7g | Fiber 1g | Sugar 9.3g | Protein 1.3g

Cashew Coconut Sauce

Prep Time: 5 minutes.

Cook Time: 0 minutes.

Serves: 6

Ingredients:

- ½ cup coconut milk
- ½ cup raw cashews
- Juice from ½ lime
- 1 ½ tablespoons red curry paste
- ¼ teaspoon salt
- 1 small garlic clove
- ½ tablespoon coco aminos

Preparation:

1. Blend cashews with lime juice and other ingredients in a blender.
2. Serve.

Serving Suggestion: Serve the sauce with baked salmon.

Variation Tip: Add crushed walnuts or pecans to the sauce.

Nutritional Information Per Serving:

Calories 97 | Fat 12g |Sodium 79mg | Carbs 8g | Fiber 1.1g | Sugar 18g | Protein 5g

Spinach Pesto

Prep Time: 5 minutes.

Cook Time: 0 minutes.

Serves: 8

Ingredients:

- 2 large handfuls spinach
- 20 basil leaves
- 1 garlic clove, peeled
- ½ lemon, squeezed
- 1 cup raw cashews
- Salt and black pepper to taste
- ¼ cup light flavor olive oil

Preparation:

1. Blend basil with garlic and other ingredients in a blender until smooth.
2. Serve.

Serving Suggestion: Serve the pesto with crispy cracker.

Variation Tip: Add crushed cocoon on top.

Nutritional Information Per Serving:

Calories 85 | Fat 14g |Sodium 122mg | Carbs 8g | Fiber 1.2g | Sugar 12g | Protein 4.3g

Bbq Sauce

Prep Time: 5 minutes.

Cook Time: 2 minutes.

Serves: 12

Ingredients:

- 6 medjool dates, pitted
- ½ cup apple juice, unsweetened
- ½ cup tomato paste
- 2 tablespoons apple cider vinegar
- ½ tablespoon Dijon mustard
- 1 teaspoon liquid smoke
- 1 teaspoon smoked paprika
- ½teaspoon garlic powder
- ½ teaspoon salt
- ½ teaspoon onion powder
- ¼ teaspoon cayenne powder

Preparation:

1. Mix mustard, dates and other ingredients in a saucepan then cook until the dates are soft.
2. Stir well and blend the mixture in a blender for 2 minutes.
3. Serve.

Serving Suggestion: Brush the sauce over beef or chicken kebabs.

Variation Tip: Add coffee power to the sauce for a strong taste.

Nutritional Information Per Serving:

Calories 159 | Fat 3g |Sodium 277mg | Carbs 9g | Fiber 1g | Sugar 9g | Protein 2g

Tartar Sauce

Prep Time: 5 minutes.

Cook Time: 0 minutes.

Serves: 8

Ingredients:

- ½ cup mayo
- 3 tablespoons dill relish, diced
- 1.5 tablespoons fresh dill
- 1 tablespoon lemon juice
- 1 teaspoon whole grain mustard
- 1 teaspoon minced garlic
- ½ teaspoon onion powder
- Salt and black pepper, to taste

Preparation:

1. Blend mayo with dill relish and other ingredients in a blender.
2. Serve.

Serving Suggestion: Serve the sauce with zucchini sushi.

Variation Tip: Add crushed nuts to the sauce.

Nutritional Information Per Serving:

Calories 118 | Fat 20g |Sodium 192mg | Carbs 6.8g | Fiber 0.9g | Sugar 19g | Protein 5.2g

30-Day Meal Plan

Week 1

Day 1:

Breakfast: Salad For Breakfast

Lunch: Potato Shredded Pork Salad

Snack: Chicken Stuffed Avocados

Dinner: Chicken Bacon Asparagus Salad

Dessert: Lime Avocado Mousse

Day 2:

Breakfast: Pizza Quiche

Lunch: Salmon Asparagus Bundles

Snack: Brussels Sprout Chips

Dinner: Skillet Roasted Chicken With Cabbage

Dessert: Chia Pudding

Day 3:

Breakfast: Sausage Balls

Lunch: Meatball Egg Soup

Snack: Buffalo Roasted Cauliflower

Dinner: Curried Pumpkin Soup

Dessert: Blueberry Cobbler

Day 4:

Breakfast: Potato Boats

Lunch: Kale Salad With Sautéed Apples

Snack: Cucumber Sushi

Dinner: Sheet Pan Chicken Fajitas

Dessert: Chocolate Pudding Cakes

Day 5:

Breakfast: Salmon Frittata

Lunch: Curried Cauliflower Rice Kale Soup

Snack: Guacamole

Dinner: Old Bay Shrimp And Sausage Sheet Pan

Dessert: Date Squares

Day 6:

Breakfast: Kale Quiche With Sweet Potato Crust

Lunch: Pulled Pork Lettuce Wraps With Avocado Aioli

Snack: California Sushi Bites

Dinner: Slow Cooker Chili

Dessert: Sautéed Apples With Caramel Drizzle

Day 7:

Breakfast: Baked Breakfast Sweet Potatoes

Lunch: Roasted Chicken Salad

Snack: Granola

Dinner: Green Curry Salmon

Dessert: Chocolate Coconut Pudding

Week 2

Day 1:

Breakfast: Salad For Breakfast

Lunch: Potato Shredded Pork Salad

Snack: Chicken Stuffed Avocados

Dinner: Chicken Bacon Asparagus Salad

Dessert: Lime Avocado Mousse

Day 2:

Breakfast: Pizza Quiche

Lunch: Salmon Asparagus Bundles

Snack: Brussels Sprout Chips

Dinner: Skillet Roasted Chicken With Cabbage

Dessert: Chia Pudding

Day 3:

Breakfast: Sausage Balls

Lunch: Meatball Egg Soup

Snack: Buffalo Roasted Cauliflower

Dinner: Curried Pumpkin Soup

Dessert: Blueberry Cobbler

Day 4:

Breakfast: Potato Boats

Lunch: Kale Salad With Sautéed Apples

Snack: Cucumber Sushi

Dinner: Sheet Pan Chicken Fajitas

Dessert: Chocolate Pudding Cakes

Day 5:

Breakfast: Salmon Frittata

Lunch: Curried Cauliflower Rice Kale Soup

Snack: Guacamole

Dinner: Old Bay Shrimp And Sausage Sheet Pan

Dessert: Date Squares

Day 6:

Breakfast: Kale Quiche With Sweet Potato Crust

Lunch: Pulled Pork Lettuce Wraps With Avocado Aioli

Snack: California Sushi Bites

Dinner: Slow Cooker Chili

Dessert: Sautéed Apples With Caramel Drizzle

Day 7:

Breakfast: Baked Breakfast Sweet Potatoes

Lunch: Roasted Chicken Salad

Snack: Granola

Dinner: Green Curry Salmon

Dessert: Chocolate Coconut Pudding

Week 3

Day 1:

Breakfast: Salad For Breakfast

Lunch: Potato Shredded Pork Salad

Snack: Chicken Stuffed Avocados

Dinner: Chicken Bacon Asparagus Salad

Dessert: Lime Avocado Mousse

Day 2:

Breakfast: Pizza Quiche

Lunch: Salmon Asparagus Bundles

Snack: Brussels Sprout Chips

Dinner: Skillet Roasted Chicken With Cabbage

Dessert: Chia Pudding

Day 3:

Breakfast: Sausage Balls

Lunch: Meatball Egg Soup

Snack: Buffalo Roasted Cauliflower

Dinner: Curried Pumpkin Soup

Dessert: Blueberry Cobbler

Day 4:

Breakfast: Potato Boats

Lunch: Kale Salad With Sautéed Apples

Snack: Cucumber Sushi

Dinner: Sheet Pan Chicken Fajitas

Dessert: Chocolate Pudding Cakes

Day 5:

Breakfast: Salmon Frittata

Lunch: Curried Cauliflower Rice Kale Soup

Snack: Guacamole

Dinner: Old Bay Shrimp And Sausage Sheet Pan

Dessert: Date Squares

Day 6:

Breakfast: Kale Quiche With Sweet Potato Crust

Lunch: Pulled Pork Lettuce Wraps With Avocado Aioli

Snack: California Sushi Bites

Dinner: Slow Cooker Chili

Dessert: Sautéed Apples With Caramel Drizzle

Day 7:

Breakfast: Baked Breakfast Sweet Potatoes

Lunch: Roasted Chicken Salad

Snack: Granola

Dinner: Green Curry Salmon

Dessert: Chocolate Coconut Pudding

Week 4

Day 1:

Breakfast: Salad For Breakfast

Lunch: Potato Shredded Pork Salad

Snack: Chicken Stuffed Avocados

Dinner: Chicken Bacon Asparagus Salad

Dessert: Lime Avocado Mousse

Day 2:

Breakfast: Pizza Quiche

Lunch: Salmon Asparagus Bundles

Snack: Brussels Sprout Chips

Dinner: Skillet Roasted Chicken With Cabbage

Dessert: Chia Pudding

Day 3:

Breakfast: Sausage Balls

Lunch: Meatball Egg Soup

Snack: Buffalo Roasted Cauliflower

Dinner: Curried Pumpkin Soup

Dessert: Blueberry Cobbler

Day 4:

Breakfast: Potato Boats

Lunch: Kale Salad With Sautéed Apples

Snack: Cucumber Sushi

Dinner: Sheet Pan Chicken Fajitas

Dessert: Chocolate Pudding Cakes

Day 5:

Breakfast: Salmon Frittata

Lunch: Curried Cauliflower Rice Kale Soup

Snack: Guacamole

Dinner: Old Bay Shrimp And Sausage Sheet Pan

Dessert: Date Squares

Day 6:

Breakfast: Kale Quiche With Sweet Potato Crust

Lunch: Pulled Pork Lettuce Wraps With Avocado Aioli

Snack: California Sushi Bites

Dinner: Slow Cooker Chili

Dessert: Sautéed Apples With Caramel Drizzle

Day 7:

Breakfast: Baked Breakfast Sweet Potatoes

Lunch: Roasted Chicken Salad

Snack: Granola

Dinner: Green Curry Salmon

Dessert: Chocolate Coconut Pudding

Conclusion

Did you like those 30-day whole foods recipes? Aren't they seem fun and easy enough to cook at home? Well, now it is time to make it all happen and enjoy a delicious meal to optimize good health. The collection of 1000 days recipes in this cookbook, along with the 30-day meal plan, will definitely help you get started with this diet. The 30-day whole foods is a month-long clean-eating plan that promises a slew of physical and mental advantages. It was created in 2009 by two qualified sports nutritionists who touted it as a means to remodel your relationship with food and reset your metabolism. The diet is based on the notion that specific food types can have a negative impact on your health and fitness. As a result, eliminating these foods from your diet should aid your body in recovering from the harmful impacts and promoting long-term health. So, let's get started!